Book Bonding

An Imagine Book
Published by Charlesbridge
9 Galen Street
Watertown, MA 02472
(617) 926-0329
www.imaginebooks.net

Library of Congress Cataloging-in-Publication Data
Names: Lambert, Megan Dowd, author. | Saine, Mia, illustrator.
Title: Book bonding: building connections through family reading / Megan Dowd Lambert;
    illustrated by Mia Saine.
Description: Watertown, MA: Charlesbridge Publishing, [2023] | Summary: "Children's
    literature educator and children's book author Megan Dowd Lambert shares a collection
    of her essays about family, reading, and bonding through books."—Provided by publisher.
Identifiers: LCCN 2021053649 (print) | LCCN 2021053650 (ebook) | ISBN 9781623541514
    (hardcover) | ISBN 9781632899279 (ebook)
Subjects: LCSH: Children—Books and reading. | Families—Books and reading. | Children's
    literature—Bibliography. | LCGFT: Essays.
Classification: LCC Z1037.A1 L224 2023 (print) | LCC Z1037.A1 (ebook) | DDC 028.5/5
    dc23/eng/20220207
LC record available at https://lccn.loc.gov/2021053649
LC ebook record available at https://lccn.loc.gov/2021053650

Printed in China
(hc) 10 9 8 7 6 5 4 3 2 1

Illustrations created digitally
Display type set in Apricot by by Rebecca Alaccari and A. R. Bosco
Text type set in Adobe Caslon Pro by Carol Twombly
Printed by 1010 Printing International Limited in Huizhou, Guangdong, China
Production supervision by Jennifer Most Delaney
Designed by Kristen Nobles

Book Bonding

BUILDING CONNECTIONS
THROUGH FAMILY READING

MEGAN DOWD LAMBERT

Illustrated by MIA SAINE

imagine!

ALSO BY MEGAN DOWD LAMBERT

For kids:

Every Day with April & Mae series, illustrated by Briana Dengoue

> *April & Mae and the Tea Party: The Sunday Book*
>
> *April & Mae and the Book Club Cake: The Monday Book*
>
> *April & Mae and the Soccer Match: The Tuesday Book*
>
> *April & Mae and the Talent Show: The Wednesday Book*
>
> *April & Mae and the Animal Shelter: The Thursday Book*

Every Day with April & Mae series, illustrated by Gisela Bohórquez

> *April & Mae and the Sleepover: The Friday Book*
>
> *April & Mae and the Movie Night: The Saturday Book*

A Crow of His Own, illustrated by David Hyde Costello

A Kid of Their Own, illustrated by Jessica Lanan

Real Sisters Pretend, illustrated by Nicole Tadgell

For adults:

> *Reading Picture Books with Children: How to Shake up Storytime and Get Kids Talking About What They See*

PLACES TO FIND MORE OF MEGAN DOWD LAMBERT'S ESSAYS

A comprehensive list is available at www.megandowdlambert.com/other-writing.

EmbraceRace, www.embracerace.org

The Horn Book, www.hbook.com

Reading While White, www.readingwhilewhite.blogspot.com

To my parents, Ray and Linda, for reading with me as a child, and to my children, Rory, Natayja, Emilia, Stevie, Caroline, Jesse, and Zachary, for reading with me as a mom

—M. D. L.

To my wonderful family, loved ones, and Memphis

—M. S.

TABLE OF CONTENTS

FOREWORD

While the *Horn Book Magazine*'s primary audience comprises librarians and teachers, we know that the books we review are intended to ultimately make their way out of libraries and schools and into the hands (and imaginations) of young people. Librarians, teachers, parents, and other adults mediate the process, but until a book is read by a child or to a child, it hasn't really come to life.

In *Book Bonding: Memories, Connections, and Family Reading*, longtime *Horn Book* contributor Megan Dowd Lambert shows us how books do come to life in what she calls her "multiracial, adoptive, queer, blended family," which includes seven children, some adoptees and some born into the family, ranging in age (at this writing) from four to twenty-five and of varying racial backgrounds. For a children's-book critic, this would seem a dream laboratory. As Megan notes, what adults want from a children's book and what children want can be very different things, so taking a book home and trying it out offers new dimensions for all concerned.

One thing that distinguishes *Book Bonding* from such favorite family-reading accounts as *Cushla and Her Books* and *How the Heather Looks* is Megan's decidedly progressive approach to both parenthood and children's literature. Despite what Fox News and right-wing talk radio might tell you, *progressive* in this instance does not mean that Megan ties her seven children to chairs for political indoctrination via *Heather Has Two Mommies*. (Although I do hope author Lesléa Newman takes pride in the fact that hers is still the go-to book that conservatives point to more than thirty years after its initial publication!) It also does not mean that Megan's approach to children's literature is a didactic one, where the primary purpose of any book is to Teach a Lesson, a basic misunderstanding of literature that plagues non-book-loving adults across the political spectrum. What I think *progressive* means in this context is this: Megan is determined to show her children the world as it is rather than the white, heterosexual, middle-class society still idealized, often unthinkingly, by too many books for young people. (The *Horn Book* sees more than five thousand new children's books a year. I know what I'm talking about.) And Megan reads with her children as a way for parent and child alike to imagine the world *as it could be.*

For Megan—and, I wish, for all parents—reading is emphatically a shared journey. She doesn't read *to* her children so much as she reads *with* them. (Although as a solitary sort, I appreciate that she gives her kids plenty of space for their own private reading.) Why read with children? There are so many reasons, but the one at the heart of this book is that "books offer a consistent means of connecting with my kids, even when (or perhaps especially when) other means fail us."

I grew up with a mother who loved to read, and what a sustaining gift that has been to me. If you are holding this book, it's a good bet that you love to read, too. Read on, and let Megan show you how to make your love for books and your love for the children in your life add up to something special.

Roger Sutton, Editor Emeritus, *The Horn Book*, Inc.
Boston, MA, 2022

PREFACE
"ON CHILDREN" . . . AND BOOKS

When our family celebrated the adoption of my first daughter, Emilia, in 2004, we played Sweet Honey in the Rock's musical adaptation of Kahlil Gibran's poem "On Children" for family and friends. It begins with these lines:

"Your children are not your children.

They are the sons and daughters of Life's longing for itself."

The words helped us acknowledge Emilia's autonomy as we celebrated her adoption into our family. We honored how she came into the world through her birth family, and we marked her place in our adoptive family. Years later, our family structure is blended and now includes nine children between my ex-wife's home and my own home. Seven are my children, and some are now young adults. Emilia is nearing adulthood, and the poem we shared at her adoption celebration still resonates with me because a central tenet of my mothering is an effort to recognize that all of my children are first and foremost their *own* people. Although part of me might rail against the separation implied by the poem-song telling me that "your children are not your children," I strive to be a mother who nurtures and supports. I want to do that even as my children realize their individual, unique potential apart from me and defined by their own thoughts, dreams, hopes, fears, strengths, struggles, and triumphs.

So how can I best bridge the distance that exists between my children and me, while I recognize and celebrate that they are their own human beings and not "mine"? How can other parents and caregivers do so, too? My multiracial, adoptive, queer, blended family life affirms that familial bonds are rooted not only in biology but in legal measures, choices, and above all, in shared experiences and love.

This is where "book bonding" comes in. I coined this phrase during my time as an educator at the Eric Carle Museum of Picture Book Art in western Massachusetts. It highlights the social and emotional impact of shared reading in classrooms and libraries. It's a happy truth that my work as an author, educator, and children's-literature scholar is deeply enriched by my life as a mother. The books on my family's bookshelves hold not just words and pictures but also memories of time spent together and of moments when reading and talking about reading have helped us better understand each other. In other words, books have helped us bond.

Time and again, shared reading has forged a common ground for my children and me as we reach toward each other across the distances between us. Witnessing my children's minds and hearts in action when we read together—or when we discuss books we read separately—gives me a greater appreciation for their individuality. This, in turn, helps me be a better parent, attuned to my kids' specific needs, strengths, and interests. For more than a decade, I've chronicled some of my family's reading life and our book bonding for the *Horn Book*; on my blog, *Book Happenings*; and on websites such as EmbraceRace and Reading While White.

I've collected and revised twenty-one pieces, introduced each to chronicle my evolving thinking, and arranged them in a sequence loosely based on themes of parenting, adoption, race, and healing conversations.

I'm convinced that the sort of book bonding that my family experiences is similar to that of anyone who reaches out to the children in their life with a book in hand. I hope my essays will enrich your family's reading and perhaps inspire you to write down some of the book-bonding memories and connections you've created when you and a child have met in the pages of a book.

Megan Dowd Lambert
Amherst, MA, 2022

PART
ONE

WORDS FOR FLORA'S MOTHER (AND OTHER IMPERFECT PARENTS)

I wrote this piece for the Horn Book *in 2014, at a point when I was feeling pretty crummy about myself as a mom. Just like reading has helped me pull myself out of low points by giving me depictions of hope, sustenance, or affirmation, writing can help me work through negative feelings. Whether I write about them or read about them, it's such a comfort to distill feelings into words—they become more manageable that way.*

Often when I mention that I have seven children, people ask, "How do you do it all?" I sometimes quote a response I heard from Dr. Donna Jo Napoli, who is a writer, professor, and mother of five: "How do I do it all? Badly. You could eat off my kitchen floor . . . for weeks."

How *I* do it all is that I don't do it all at once. As I sit down to write, my kitchen is a mess and some of my kids are at their other house with their other mom. I miss my children when they're not with me, but I'm also grateful to be able to work like hell on the days they're gone and then really focus on them when they're at our home.

Shared reading enables us to slow down and enjoy one another's company in the midst of our busy, transition-laden routines. Soon after it came out, I read Kate DiCamillo and K. G. Campbell's 2014 Newbery Medal winner, *Flora & Ulysses: The Illuminated Adventures*, with four of my children. I read the advance reading copy first and knew my kids would be pulled in by the exact elements that made me initially skeptical. A superhero squirrel? Quasi-comic-book art? Not my cup of tea. But I also felt myself yearning to deliver the message of unconditional love that's at the heart of the book: "Nothing would be easier without you."

Sometimes I worry that my kids might think I feel like life *would* be easier without them. There are days when I snap or I'm grouchy or just plain overwhelmed by my inability to balance work and motherhood. DiCamillo's novel made me think about children's literature's less-than-ideal parents and what they communicate about family life to child and adult readers. I don't mean Roald Dahlian parents like poor Matilda Wormwood's dreadful mother and father, but more like Flora's divorced parents or her friend William Spiver's mother and "her new husband." These secondary, or even offstage, adult characters are believable in all their flawed humanity. Flora grapples with the shortcomings of the adults in her life, but DiCamillo paints her characters with such subtlety that the lesson doesn't overwhelm the story.

On the flip side, many books have a mommy or daddy who endlessly reassures their little Stinky Face or Nutbrown Hare about their "love-you-forever" love. These don't reflect the times we parents fail, as Flora's mother does. They instead present us with visions of what we might be on our best days.

It's the rare person who rises to the level of the idealized parenting achieved, for example, by the father in Mo Willems's picture book *Knuffle Bunny Too: A Case of Mistaken Identity*. When daughter Trixie realizes in the middle of the night that she took home the wrong Knuffle, Daddy agrees to an on-the-spot stuffed-bunny exchange. Would I do such a thing? Not a chance. Faced with such a scenario, I'd tell my kid that we'd sort things out in the morning. If I were feeling very generous, I'd tuck her back in with another stuffed animal. And with apologies to Kate Banks and Georg Hallensleben and their lovely picture book *And If the Moon Could Talk*, I wouldn't go back and forth in a reverie about celestial bodies' communication or whatever. Good. Night.

And yet, even if I don't aspire to Trixie's daddy's selflessness, I absolutely see a reflection of myself in how exhausted he looks when Trixie rouses him from a deep sleep. Indeed, some of the most rounded portraits of parents in picture books come in stories about them trying to get their little ones, in the immortal words of Adam Mansbach, to "go the f*ck to sleep." Amy Schwartz's *Some Babies*, David Ezra Stein's *Interrupting Chicken*, and Janet S. Wong and John Wallace's *Grump* are just a few that conclude with beleaguered, fatigued parents nodding off while trying (and failing) to put their kids to bed.

Why are they so tired? Well, because the days leading up to those fraught bedtimes can be . . . long. I have a soft spot in my heart for how Marla Frazee depicts a little girl's exasperated mother in *Harriet, You'll Drive Me Wild!* by Mem Fox; a beleaguered Mrs. Peters who can't satisfy everyone's tastes in *The Seven Silly Eaters* by Mary Ann Hoberman; and the not-so-flattering but oh-so-familiar portrayals of parents at the mercy of their *Boss Baby*. And high on my list of illustrations that show the tedium of daily routines is a vignette from Amy Schwartz's slice-of-life picture book *A Glorious Day*. The droll text reads: "At home Henry and his mother play trains. Henry is the big train, and his mother is the small train. All morning long." I can practically hear Henry's mother meditating on a refrain from another train book—"I think I can, I think I can"—as she puts in quality floor time with her kid. And yet she's hanging in there.

The same cannot be said of Flora's mother in DiCamillo's novel. She's so wrapped up in herself and her career as a romance novelist that she seems oblivious to her daughter's needs. She might find kinship with the mother of another Flora, the star of Jeanne Birdsall and Matt Phelan's picture book *Flora's Very Windy Day*. I've read it with my children and recognize myself in its depiction of a mother driven to weary despair as she shoos them outside while trying to get some work done. Is she writing a romance novel on that laptop on the very first spread? I don't know. But I do know that she, like me sometimes, is not having a terribly glorious day of attentive mothering.

In *Flora's Very Windy Day*, Phelan's art deftly and powerfully conveys emotional conflict. On the first double-page spread, Flora is on the left, Eloise-like in her rage, with red squiggles and lines surrounding her. Little brother Crispin sits at a safe distance by a messy art table (on the dedication page, he spills his sister's paints—again!), his sidelong gaze directed at Flora. He's clearly seen her blow her top before. Their mother is far to the right, turning away from her computer screen with a wan, defeated expression. While Flora is unquestionably the focus—eyes are on her, and her outraged stance demands attention—I can't help but home in on her mother. I know her. I've *been* her. I want to give her a hug.

When we read this book together, did my children notice this mom? Not really. And who can blame them? Flora is a force to be reckoned with, and my kids are much more interested in sibling conflict. When they *did* shift their attention to the mother, it was to remark, "It's not fair!" when she insists Flora take Crispin outside with her. "Give her a break!" I said in a mothers-of-the-world-unite sort of way.

The wind carries Crispin away, and Flora resolves to retrieve him: "My mother wouldn't like it if I lost him." My daughter Emilia empathetically piped up, "And Flora would miss him, too, even if he spills her paints." On the penultimate spread, Flora and Crispin return home. Their mother, channeling Max's mom in Maurice Sendak's *Where the Wild Things Are* with "still hot" dinner, has chocolate chip cookies ready. The story could end there (the text does), but Phelan delivers heartwarming images on the final page that shift attention away from the mother's act of apology and back to the sibling dynamic. The pictures show Flora and Crispin sitting apart and eating their cookies, then leaning into each other, not making eye contact or smiling, but with a closeness between their little bodies that communicates forgiveness. The scene is familiar to me, both as an older sister and as a mother. Children bicker and make up, love one another through and despite the times when they fail or hurt or disappoint one another. "Nothing would be easier without you," these pictures seem to say, "even if you spill my paints."

Child readers typically aren't interested in a mother's emotional story arc, and I appreciate that this ending isn't about Flora and Crispin's mother's apology. I recall with chagrin one time when I was sick with the flu—and also sick of kids bickering before bedtime. Instead of letting my children choose our reading material, I dramatically pulled William Steig's *Brave Irene* off the shelf. I self-indulgently noted how its intrepid child protagonist lavishes her ill mother with affection and support.

"Oh, Mom-Mom," Emilia said after I'd read a few pages, "we have not been so nice as Irene."

Did that make me feel any better? Of course not. I felt like a jerk. Guilt-tripping one's children into sympathy through passive-aggressive bedtime reading isn't a terrific parenting strategy. I can report, however, that my other kids weren't so moved. "You're not really *that* sick," Stevie said. "Can I choose the next book?" Caroline asked. And on we went.

I know my kids will recall that their childhood—though filled with books, and play, and each other, and parents in two houses who adore them—was not just overflowing with wonder and whimsy but also included parenting failures. And I know that my own faults contribute to some of the less-than-ideal moments they'll remember. That was a hard pill to swallow as I reread DiCamillo's book and anticipated Flora's reconciliation with her mother. I've come to think that the resolution may be a comfort to child readers who see Flora confirm her mother's love, and it also gently guides them toward accepting flawed adults. Forgive them, books such as these seem to say; we know precisely what they do, and we bet they feel like crap about it.

DiCamillo's novel avoids having the final words delivered in a parental voice begging filial pardon. Instead, the closing poem is the superhero squirrel's affirmation of his devotion to the girl who saved him. Adoptive parents like me frequently encounter well-intentioned but misguided comments implying that we saved our kids. "They're so lucky to have you," is the refrain, belying the core losses that premise adoption. The truism that my kids' other mom and I often resort to is that *we* are the lucky ones, since our children accepted us as their parents. Nothing would be harder to imagine than life without them. Paraphrasing DiCamillo: "It's a miracle. Or something."

And if I ever lose sight of the miracle of this modern family of mine, there's nothing like settling in with a book. It helps redirect my family's attention away from the tumult of our own foibles and failings toward the common ground of others' stories. Book bonding, I call it. We put aside quarrels over who had more time on the Xbox, why it's so hard to bring the freaking laundry downstairs, and whatever is "not fair!" at any given moment.

Together we read about everything from very windy days to bunny-exchanging daddies to mothers driven wild to superhero squirrels. And holy bagumba, as Flora might say, we create book bonds. I'll love those times forever—to the moon and back! The kitchen floor can wait.

READING ABOUT FAMILY
IN MY FAMILY

This was my first Horn Book *essay, published in 2008. I'm forever grateful to author Jacqueline Woodson for emailing me after she read it to thank me for championing queer-inclusive children's literature. This revised version gives a nod to Woodson's own role in depicting diverse family constellations and reissues the call for greater progress. I think an essential ingredient to book bonding is the experience of seeing one's own family reflected in books.*

I've yet to find a children's book with a cast of characters that looks like my multiracial, foster-adoptive, queer, blended family, and I know there are lots of artistic, social, political, and market-driven reasons for that. When my oldest (a biracial, biological son) was my only child, I took children's-literature scholar Dr. Rudine Sims Bishop's metaphor about books acting as "windows, mirrors, and sliding glass doors" (which she first introduced in 1990 in an article in *Perspectives*) to heart. I scoured libraries, bookstores, and book lists to try to find my son books that would provide not only windows into others' experiences but mirrors of his own, while allowing him to step into other worlds and possibilities through his reading. Much to my chagrin, and despite my best efforts to find books to reflect his family, Rory didn't seem to care very much that Heather had two mommies or that "black is brown is tan," to quote Arnold Adoff and Emily Arnold McCully's classic picture book. He was far more interested in Captain Underpants and Sylvester and his magic pebble, thank you very much.

I had the good intention of wanting to provide my son with a literary world that reflected the life experiences we shared as a multiracial, two-mom family in a diverse community of friends and neighbors. But while my son was included in that world, he also had a world of his own devising. He was growing up and developing his own identity; making his own friends; following his own passions, tastes, and interests; and formulating his own visions for his future. After all, my son's world, occupied as it was by the stuff of preschool, was also one in which he imagined the adult he would become. Once while reading *Homemade Love* by bell hooks and Shane W. Evans, Rory said something along the lines of "I like reading this book about a family with all Brown people because maybe someday I will grow up and have a family like that, too." Eureka! I exhaled alongside overburdened Heather and her mommies and the "black is brown is tan" family and realized that Rory had a point. Reading children's books isn't all about looking at the here and now. It can also be about envisioning the up ahead and later.

Growing up is not a tragedy; it's a birthright. If a main task of childhood is to leave it, then children's books can help support empowered leave-taking and resist the nostalgia that society often attaches to childhood. Such support is eroded, however, when children don't see themselves and their experiences reflected in their books. Following such a line of thinking offers another argument for children's books that include queer adults: they affirm kids raised by queer parents and queer kids themselves. After all, a queer child raised by straight parents would be well served by a book that depict families with two mommies or two daddies, since they may see their own future in it, right?

Of course, there are limits to this vision of aspirational children's literature based in a child's perceptions of adulthood. When Rory announced that he was going to marry his preschool friends Andy, Tim, and Rose, I didn't think he was precociously coming out as a bisexual polyamorist. What I understood from his declaration was that Rory really liked his friends. A preschooler doesn't get what marriage is because it's an adult institution. That's why when *King & King* by Linda de Haan and Stern Nijland came out (as it were), I felt that it was a book aimed more at well-intentioned, anti-homophobic adults than at children. And yet, even if Rory's notions about marriage were a bit muddled, they didn't conform to heteronormativity. I'm sure that his lived experience with two moms and with friends who also had queer parents informed him, and I bet the queer books on his shelves (though few in number) did, too. To stretch an aphorism: children are our future, but they're also our present.

Fast-forward a couple of decades, and my work on the curation team of OurShelves (a book-box subscription to encourage publishers to offer more inclusive, diverse content in children's books through customer demand) gives me reason to hope. But change is happening very slowly. In 2017, lesbian friends asked me for picture books depicting families awaiting the birth of a baby to read to their then two-year-old. I could find only two titles that didn't include a mommy and a daddy: Jacqueline Woodson and Sophie Blackall's *Pecan Pie Baby*, with its depiction of a single expectant mother and her daughter within a warm extended family and community, and John Burningham and Helen Oxenbury's *There's Going to Be a Baby*, which follows a little boy and his mother imagining what the new baby in their family will be like and then introduces a grandfather arriving when the mother goes to the hospital.

This experience is just one reason why I'm always on the lookout for books that depict different kinds of families and different ways of being in the world. I like to think that Heather and her mommies have made room for more of their friends, too.

IN DEFENSE OF GENTLE MEN

When my ex-wife and I both ended up with male partners, our kids got some truly excellent stepdads. Their presence in our lives made me think more deeply about depictions of men as nurturers, particularly as my husband, Sean, and I anticipated our son Jesse's birth as baby number six in the family. I wrote this essay for the Horn Book *in 2015 to ask, What do books say to kids about masculinity and gender norms?*

I admit that I've mourned favorite picture books that didn't make the Caldecott Awards cut, among them Marla Frazee's *The Farmer and the Clown* (now the first book in a three-part series about these characters). I'd given a copy to my daughter Caroline, and my initial liking deepened into outright adoration through our shared reading.

"Look how the farmer teaches the clown-kid farm things, and the clown teaches the farmer clown things. But the farmer messes up the juggling, and that's funny," Caroline noted.

Later she expanded her analysis of Frazee's complex and complementary characterizations: "How this book works is—it's like he's happy but then really sad," she said, pointing to the clown. "And like he's sad but then is really happy," she concluded with respect to the farmer. In other words, appearances are deceptive, and a happy face can mask inner pain, as surely as a gruff exterior can obscure a heart of gold.

I've long admired Frazee's work, and I had high hopes that this picture book might be the one that would propel her from two-time Caldecott Honor status to Caldecott medalist. To me it's the whole package—a remarkable feat of wordless storytelling, a rich visual experience, and an emotionally powerful and satisfying narrative.

Clearly the Caldecott committee that year didn't agree.

Having served on one of these committees, I can attest to the integrity of the process. It's a collaborative effort in which many voices and perspectives weigh in and come to agreement, and I know from experience that some favorite books don't rise to the top. Due to the confidentiality of deliberations, we'll never know why Frazee's (brilliant!) book didn't make the cut for the medal, nor for one of the six (six is a lot!) honors in its year. Rumblings outside the committee room, on the internet, and in a mock Caldecott session I oversaw suggest a very sorry reason that some people didn't feel the love for this particular book, one that never came up in my daughter Caroline's readings. (I'm not pointing fingers at selection committee members here.)

I'm not talking about coulrophobia. Reactions based on how "creepy" clowns are didn't stick in my craw. What did were comments about the perceived "creepy" dynamic between the farmer (described by Caroline as "kind and nice") and the young clown. The mock Caldecott debate was the first place I encountered this perception. A participant suggested that others (not necessarily she) might take issue with the scenes of an older, solitary man sitting by the bedside of a young, vulnerable child.

Whaaaat? I wanted to say.

I just couldn't see how the farmer could be read as predatory. Gruff (at first), sure . . . but a threat to this little clown-kid?

No. Way.

Our culture persists in viewing older, solitary, and (I would add) gentle men as threats. It's a pernicious viewpoint that smacks of rigid gender roles (real men aren't nurturers, so there must be some sinister motivation behind the farmer's caring demeanor) and homophobia (why is this guy alone, and where's the lady, the angel of the house, to keep him in check?). It makes me want to get on the nearest soapbox. Don't get me wrong— I know that some children suffer terrible abuse at the hands of men. I don't deny or minimize this awful truth. It's the knee-jerk equating of an older, solitary, gentle man with predator that troubles me.

I heard similar suggestions after the Caldecott committee I sat on named *A Sick Day for Amos McGee* as the medalist. In several conversations with my students, Amos was deemed "creepy." To my bafflement, he was likened to Mister Rogers—in a *bad* way. Now I admit that I have a real soft spot for Fred Rogers. I grew up loving his show. My husband and I asked my uncle who officiated our wedding to quote him in the service. I naively hadn't realized the vitriol, or at least mistrust, with which some regard him—saying he comes across as a pedophile.

Whaaat? I wanted to say (again).

But a teacher doesn't say such things if she wants her students to think through assumptions. So as my class talked about Amos McGee that year, I asked, "Tell me more. Why do you think Mister Rogers is 'creepy'? Or Amos?"

The gentle, nurturing attributes of these solitary, older male characters quickly came to the forefront of our discussion. While steering these classes to consider gender norms and their limiting power, I was nevertheless repeatedly heartbroken—not just for Amos or Mister Rogers or Frazee's farmer, but also for the many wonderfully gentle, older, solitary men in the real world, and on behalf of the children they nurture.

I find myself determined to rise up in defense of them. I want to highlight more like them in children's literature to assert their rightful—and, I would argue, crucial—place in children's (reading) lives. I'm particularly invested in this as the mother of sons who need and deserve diverse models of masculinity, and as the mother of children with not one but two stepfathers.

My ex-wife's partner, Ramsey, is a loving, playful, energetic sort who evokes the type of fatherly spirit found in Bob Shea's *Oh, Daddy!* He tussles with the kids and delights in roughhouse play and open physical affection. Meanwhile, my husband, Sean, makes me think of all those thoughtful, patient, gentle mouse dads in Kevin Henkes's picture books like *Chrysanthemum*, letting the kids come to him and greeting them with open arms. "I always wanted a dad," my son Stevie whispered when Sean tucked him into bed the night we announced our engagement. A playful male caregiver seems more culturally celebrated, but surely there's room for a gentle fatherly figure, too?

It seems that dads often feature in stories in which a gruff man turns gentle over time. And it seems that in the case of solitary, older-men characters, this change is fraught for some readers who worry that the evolution is somehow suspect. Peers of Frazee's gruff turned-gentle farmer abound in other picture books. Perhaps my favorite is found in the middle of a city during the Great Depression in Sarah Stewart and David Small's *The Gardener*. Little Lydia Grace melts the heart of crotchety bachelor Uncle Jim, and I have a hard time getting through it without tearing up at the sight of his goodbye to her at the book's end. Might others regard his hug as . . . too much? Or his earlier kindnesses as problematic?

Other men in children's books needn't be transformed to display remarkable generosity and kindness to children, because these are their defining attributes. Two nameless characters come immediately to mind: the man who tosses Max the drumsticks at the end of Brian Pinkney's *Max Found Two Sticks* and the one who gives Ben a trumpet at the conclusion of Rachel Isadora's *Ben's Trumpet*. These are quick, resolved interactions between characters, the men appearing for wish fulfillment and to satisfyingly conclude the boys' stories. But in light of some responses to Amos, Frazee's farmer, and Mister Rogers, might some regard these acts as incidents of stranger danger?

Far more dangerous, it seems to me, is a lack of interrogation of the cultural forces that could lead readers to perceive such men as threats. Men's nurturing roles in children's lives are not only potentially beneficial, they are also liberating for women, long expected to be the primary (if not sole) nurturers.

From my perch up here on my soapbox, I'll cheer on diverse examples of masculinity in books for young readers and continue to rail against anything that deems the farmer or Amos or Mister Rogers as "creepy." I'm not saying that all these books deserve medals for the ways they push against gender norms, but surely such characterization should not be cited as a reason not to recommend or reward a book.

Years after its publication, *The Farmer and the Clown* remains one of Caroline's favorite picture books. "I love how the pictures tell the whole story," she said to me one day. "All the details show you what's going on, but you get to figure it out yourself." Her appreciation for how wordless picture books inherently trust readers to make meaning of illustrations made me realize anew the genius of Frazee's work. A story that is all about building trust between characters trusts its readers to deduce its visual storytelling. There's risk in that trust—borne out by readings that vilify the farmer—but my daughter's moving readings make the most of it.

"Tell me more," I asked her. "What specifically do you like about the story?"

"Well, I guess it's mostly that the clown is so different from the farmer, but the farmer doesn't judge. And he doesn't just leave the clown there. He stays with the clown and makes the clown feel safe."

With this reflection on the characters' dynamic, I see the depths of my daughter's compassion. She sees two characters, markedly different from each other, who form a bond. She sees a smaller, vulnerable character made to feel safe and helped by a bigger, gruffer one. She sees possibility for how we can bring out the best in each other.

It's a worldview some may consider naive or even risky, but it's one that her other mom, her gentle stepdads, and I value tremendously in our daughter.

DRAWN TOGETHER
BY PICTURE BOOKS

This piece began as a post for the Horn Book's *annual* Calling Caldecott *blog in 2018. Some of the most important people in my children's lives have been their teachers. Reading* Drawn Together *with my son and talking about it with his teacher enhanced my appreciation for how a book about bonding through art reflexively invites its readers to bond through reading it together.*

I was instantly intrigued when illustrator Dan Santat described on social media how he developed the display type for *Drawn Together*, written by Minh Lê. He wrote, "It originates from the original Thai alphabet. Then I integrated Western alphabet components into the design to show a melding of cultures. Lastly, for design reasons, I modified certain characters for legibility."

This typographic cultural melding offers an immediate, visual representation of the connection forged by the story's English-speaking boy and his Thai-speaking grandfather when they transcend language barriers through art. I mentioned Santat's intentions at a presentation I led at my youngest sons' preschool using the storytime model I developed in association with the Eric Carle Museum of Picture Book Art, the Whole Book Approach.

Afterward, my son Jesse's teacher Will thanked me for all I'd taught him about typography, endpapers, book jackets, page layout, and so on. Then his tone changed, and he said, "I hope this isn't oversharing, but I want to say that as you were talking, I kept thinking about my mom. She read with us all the time." His voice caught as he continued, "She died last year, right after my son was born, and she would've loved all these books."

I said the first thing that came to mind: "And now whenever you read with your son, it'll be a way of making your mom present in his life. And it'll let you reconnect with your memories of reading with her."

Will smiled. "Wow. I feel like I just went to therapy. Really good therapy," he said with a little laugh as he held fast to the truth that shared reading could draw him and his son together with his much-missed mom.

I thought of Will and his family when I realized the dual meaning of *Drawn Together*: the characters *draw together* and in doing so are emotionally *drawn together*. Clever, right? But this picture book's brilliance is in how it can draw readers together, too.

When I read the book with Jesse, he repeatedly changed his mind about what was "*really* happening" in the scenes with the monkey, the fish, and the dragon images that seem to come to life from the grandfather and grandson's drawings.

"Is this real?" he kept asking.

Then "I think it's real!"

And then "No, I think it's just their pictures. But their pictures *are* real!"

And then, uncertainly, "Right, Mommy?"

I loved seeing his mind at work, so I resisted giving him my own interpretations and instead held space for his questions. When we turned the last page, Jesse saw that the back endpapers show the grandfather's line drawings, and he delightedly flipped back to the front ones to confirm that they employ the boy's art style. We removed the jacket to discover a twist that made Jesse gasp, momentarily "speechless" (like the characters) as he realized that the cover looks just like the grandfather's black sketchbook.

"It *is* real!" said Jesse. "*This* is the grandpa's book of drawings! So the whole book is real!"

I understood Jesse's delight in the metafictive blurring of his own world and the world of the book. It was connected to his earlier attempts to navigate the ambiguous scenes at the heart of this story. Are these pictures that the pair have "drawn together"? Or are they a metaphorical dreamscape of sorts? Is this a fantastical realm that they, as wizard and warrior, negotiate? Just like Lê's text leaves room for Santat's art to extend the story visually, the merging of the visual and the verbal gives readers space to grapple with the meaning(s) of these scenes.

And it's through such grappling that readers can connect not just with story and art but with each other. That's what I meant when I told Will that he could connect himself and his son with his late mom through shared reading. Picture books hold not just words and illustrations but memories. The three of them will never read *Drawn Together* together. But when and if Will shares it with his son, he will draw on the experiences of his childhood shared readings with his mom, recreating past book bonding as he bonds through books with his child.

WAITING TO SEE
WHAT WILL HAPPEN NEXT

This was the first post I wrote for the Horn Book's Calling Caldecott *blog. I was missing my eldest child, Rory, who had just started his first year of college in 2015. He's graduated and living on his own now, but I still encounter books that make me think of him—whether or not we ever read them together.*

When I first read *Waiting* by Kevin Henkes, it made me think of my oldest son, Rory. At two or three years old, he used to create what his other mom and I called "altars." We'd walk into his bedroom or the kitchen or living room and find graceful little arrangements of toys and other objects he'd gathered from around the house. Visits to the playground often resulted in altars made of stones, acorns, pine cones, and sandbox toys. It was as if he were a pint-sized installation artist bent on creating order and balance from found objects.

I thought of Rory's altars when I saw Henkes's illustration in *Waiting* on a page with text that says, "Sometimes there were gifts." The five toys on the windowsill behold an assortment of small objects: an acorn, a marble, a shell. This scene was akin to the altars Rory created and watched over.

Why were these displays so vital to him? I think part of their importance arose from being a site of control. Children exercise very little power in their lives. They start off as utterly helpless and vulnerable infants, and only slowly and haphazardly do they gain agency and control over their day-to-day existence. There is no child in Henkes's picture book, but the toys arranged on the windowsill imply a child's hand and control, and the design of the book invites a child reader to actively participate in a shared reading.

Reading *Waiting* on my own, I appreciated Henkes's fearless use of white space. I marveled at how he seemed to channel one of Rory's favorite artists, James Marshall, who had the ability to convey expression with mere dots and lines for eyes and mouths on his hippopotamus characters, George and Martha. I delighted in the expert pacing of the text and in the wordless spreads that evoke a quiet, contemplative wild rumpus.

After I read *Waiting* in a Whole Book Approach storytime at the Eric Carle Museum of Picture Book Art, I emerged even more convinced that it was a Caldecott contender. When I asked the storytime group what they saw on the jacket, one child immediately noticed that the toys are gazing out the window at clouds that reflect their shapes. Then I showed them the back of the jacket, and they noticed the toy cat.

"It's not on the front," one child observed.

"It's not there, either," said another child when I turned to the title page.

The dedication page shows the three "gifts" that show up later in the story, and the children simply named them when we encountered them on this early page. Ultimately naming them proved useful in recollecting them, and a child burst out, "Maybe that's what they're waiting for!" in direct reference to the title.

A similar response came when the "cat with patches joined them."

"I was *waiting* for that cat!" someone exclaimed.

Here I plainly saw how well Henkes knows his child audience. As many reviewers noted, waiting is central to a child's existence, and this ties into Rory's lack of control I mentioned earlier. But what this storytime underscored is that it's not only the characters who wait. Child readers wait during a reading, too. Sometimes the payoff is a fulfillment of expectation of the gifts and the cat introduced early on. And readers also await small twists that result in unexpected occurrences—the quasi-birth of the nesting-doll cat's kittens, the sight of the toys stiffly prone on the windowsill when they sleep, the tragic fall of the elephant.

"I think that rabbit pushed him," one child said, instantly sparking a storytime debate reminiscent of *I Want My Hat Back* throwdowns I've mediated in the past about whether the bear eats the rabbit at the end. Like Jon Klassen, Henkes trusts his child readers. He doesn't push morals or tidy messages on them. He just lets them *wait* to see what will happen—what will change, what will arrive, what will come to be.

If we want to identify a message in *Waiting*, I think we can find one that verges on the holy. This book quietly asserts that there are gifts to be had in waiting and in the realization of answers that culminate in periods of wonder.

Time moves so quickly. The little boy who made altars in my home and on the playground is now an adult who still loves to read and who is engaged in a wide range of creative pursuits, from acting to photography and from writing to sound design and music. We both waited his whole life for his growth into independence, and now our visits and conversations always leave me excitedly "waiting to see what would happen next."

PART
TWO

HOME SECURITY

This essay was first published in the Horn Book *in 2009 and is about my eldest daughter, Natayja, who is now a young adult. Picture books began my book bonding with her when she first came home to our family, and one story in particular,* The Three Little Pigs, *stands out in my memory as a tale that helped me connect with her.*

When my daughter Natayja was ten years old, she turned the corner from reluctant reader to—if not an avid reader like her older brother, Rory—an *interested* reader.

"May I please stay up just fifteen more minutes to finish this book?" she asked one night, clutching a copy of Jeff Smith's *Bone* to her chest.

To quote one little red hen, "And she did."

Natayja's journey to this exciting new stage in her reading life was a circuitous one. She was raised by her biological mother (or "first mother," as we sometimes say in our family) for most of the first six years of her life. Although enough went wrong to land Natayja and her little brother, Stevie, in the foster care system when she was a kindergartener and he was just two months old, an awful lot went right, too. She emerged as a resilient, loving, and openhearted child. I first met her when she was seven, after she had lived in several foster homes, often separated from Stevie. A year later, she and Stevie came home to our family in a pre-adoptive foster placement.

I was already mother to three other children at that point in my life: one biological son, Rory, and two daughters, Emilia and Caroline, who'd come home to our family through the foster system as newborns. As I welcomed Natayja and Stevie into my heart and my home, I was nervous about what it would be like to bond with children who had life history outside of our family. But just as reading aloud with my three babies helped set the stage for attachment, shared reading with Natayja and Stevie provided first steps toward bonding with them. After all, reading with children isn't only about oral transmission of text and beholding of art, it can also be about creating a common ground for connecting with one another through words, pictures, and shared time and space. While getting to know the characters in books we've shared, we've also gotten to know each other.

It didn't much matter what Natayja and I read. The simple act of curling up with books was enough. While she was leery of hugs and kisses and other moments of physical closeness, she still clamored to sit close enough to see pictures well and to silently read along with me. 'Twas the season when she and Stevie came home, so we read all the Christmas books in the house. We also began to make our way steadily through fairy tales (she didn't know many), nursery rhymes (ditto), and countless picture books.

One story in particular grabbed Natayja's attention: *The Three Little Pigs*. We read every version in our house and then looked for more at the library. David Wiesner's postmodern fractured version, *The Three Pigs*, was a particular favorite, but she also loved Margot Zemach's more classic fare and Barry Moser's darker retelling. Jon Scieszka and Lane Smith's humor in *The True Story of the 3 Little Pigs* tickled her funny bone, and she loved the shifted perspective offered by Eugene Trivizas and Helen Oxenbury's *The Three Little Wolves and the Big Bad Pig*.

Natayja didn't simply enjoy this story by reading it with me and on her own—she also drew pictures of the characters and their houses, acted it out with dolls, blocks, and other toys, and staged mini-performances with her brothers and sisters. One day during a routine therapy appointment that was part of her transition into our family, Natayja began building three houses out of blocks from a basket in the doctor's office.

"They're the three pigs' houses," she announced.

"She loves that story," I told the therapist.

"Well, that makes sense, doesn't it?" she replied. "It's all about making a safe home."

I sat there dumbstruck. Here, made plain before my eyes, was the power and potential of story. I often fret about finding good books that explicitly address foster care, adoption, and how love makes a family, and I will always be on the lookout—and grateful—for books that do this well. But here was an example of a child finding a story that spoke to her both powerfully and subtly.

Rest assured, we didn't make anything more of Natayja's play that day. We didn't ask her to talk about the connections in her life, moving from one home to the next, worrying about her brother when they were apart, and facing too many wolves at too many doors. We just watched her play. And in watching her, I got to know my new daughter better that day as a child who can dig deep into stories, art, make-believe, and her very self in order to grapple with the stuff of life.

I am not advocating that readers rigidly cast *The Three Little Pigs* as a metaphor for children who have experienced foster care. Instead, I relate this story as a way of exploring how children's reading experiences can push beyond authorial intent and parental expectations. Reviewer Joanna Rudge Long read a post I wrote about Natayja and *The Three Little Pigs*, and she referenced it in her March 2009 essay in the *Horn Book* about different versions of the story. She wrote, "One newly adopted eight-year-old's favorite story is *The Three Little Pigs*, which she explored in many editions. Perhaps *The Three Little Pigs* speaks so eloquently to this young veteran of foster care because it's about finding a secure home."

I think the word *perhaps* is important here. It's entirely possible that Natayja didn't consciously or even unconsciously draw the connections between her life and this story, and I had no interest in huffing and puffing them at her. I just wanted to keep encouraging her on her own path as an independent reader while continuing to read stories aloud with her, because I'm convinced they're a crucial part of the stuff that will guide, inspire, and sustain her as she builds her own story.

HOW *UNIDENTIFIED SUBURBAN OBJECT* HELPED MY KIDS CLAIM SUBJECTIVITY

Reading Mike Jung's middle-grade novel Unidentified Suburban Object *with two of my children was a rich, rewarding experience. I wrote two posts about it for the* EmbraceRace *blog in 2016, and I've edited and adapted them into this single, shorter piece. Although Jung's story isn't about transracial adoption, it provided entry points for my kids and me to talk about their experiences as children of color in our family and in the broader world, allowing me to better support them and see them in their experiences.*

When I started hearing buzz about Mike Jung's *Unidentified Suburban Object*, I moved it to the top of my list of books to read with my children Stevie and Caroline. It ended up giving us one of the most meaningful shared reading experiences I've ever had as a mom. A favorite moment occurred during a big reveal when the middle-school-aged protagonist, Chloe Cho, discovers that her parents' life story isn't what they'd always told her. When I read the scene with Chloe's revelation about her heritage with my kids, Stevie shook his head back and forth, as if rattling his brain around in his skull, and said, "Wait. What?! Really?"

"So that means *she's* . . . ?" asked Caroline.

They were riveted.

I hope a lot of readers will get to discover the book's plot twist on their own, so I won't spoil it here. But even if you know about it ahead of time, there's much to be savored and appreciated in Jung's book beyond its stunning reveal. For one thing, it includes some of the most fearless and seamless accounts of a child of color confronting race-based microaggressions that I've ever encountered. The story was both entertaining and great fodder for conversation about my kids' lives, because reading about Chloe's righteous indignation and empowered responses to others' assumptions, slights, and wrongdoing in *Unidentified Suburban Object* let us talk about how Caroline and Stevie confront similar situations.

"That was so *rude*!" Caroline exclaimed when we read a scene in which Chloe blows up at a teacher after his unrelenting comparisons of her to a famous Korean American musical prodigy.

"Yeah, but he was rude, too," said Stevie, and there was a certain admiration in his voice for Chloe and her fearless, outspoken response.

"True!" said Caroline. "Keep reading, Mom-Mom." And I did.

I've read some online reviews calling Chloe Cho "unlikeable," but I love her. When Stevie and Caroline cheered her on, not *despite* her sharp edges and fierce resolve but *because* of them, I said a silent thanks to Mike Jung for giving my kids this spirited protagonist. Do I want my kids to be rude? No. Do I hope they will respond to others with patience, compassion, dignity, openness, and curiosity? Yes. Do I realize that the stakes are high for kids of color speaking out against authority? Absolutely. I carry all of these convictions with me as I center a primary concern for my children's wholeness rather than protecting the feelings of people who are insensitive or worse.

Caroline's appearance often provokes comments about her fashion sense and her gender-bending presentation. After she campaigned successfully to get her first shaved-sides hairdo when she entered kindergarten, I told her to expect comments and questions.

"If someone says something about your hair, how will you respond?"

"If it's a nice thing, I'll say, 'Thanks. I like your hair, too.' If it's not nice, I'll say, 'You hurt my feelings when you said that.'"

It was a start.

Soon after the first day of school, my mother was with Caroline at a local playground and a little girl asked, "Are you a boy or a girl?"

Caroline responded, "A girl."

"Then why does your hair look like that?" the girl followed up, and Caroline paused, not sure what to say.

My mother piped up and said, "Because she's a rock star!"

Affirmed, Caroline beamed and said, "Yeah. I just like my hair like this."

"Oh, that's nice," said the girl. "Do you want to play with me?"

And off they went. This was a pretty ideal exchange, and it wasn't an instance of race-based microaggression, although it could have veered into territory in which Caroline's gender nonconformity was not the subject of friendly curiosity but of scrutiny or degradation. The other girl was open and kind, and Caroline felt supported by her grandmother and able to confidently assert herself as a rock star—a girl who likes what she likes.

I used this story to talk with Caroline about another sort of question she might encounter as a biracial person whom others struggle to identify in terms of race or ethnicity.

"Remember when that little girl asked if you were a girl or a boy, and Linney (my kids' name for their grandmother) said, 'She's a rock star'?"

"Yeah."

"Has anyone ever asked you, 'What are you?'" I asked her.

"What do you mean?" she replied.

"Like when they are trying to figure out more about you? Like your race?"

"I don't know. If anyone asked me, 'What are you?' I think I'd just say I am a girl who's nine."

"What would you say about your race? Would you say African American or Black, or Brown, or biracial, or something else?"

"I would say I'm African American. But 'What are you?' is a weird question."

I think Caroline's resistance to this careless but common question with the comment that it's "weird" is a way of calling out how it makes her feel othered—in other words, how it functions as a microaggression. I want my kids to be able to respond to such queries in ways that make them feel less like unidentified objects and more like empowered kids of color like Chloe Cho. One approach I've offered my kids is an "ask back" strategy I once read about, which levels the conversation by placing both parties as active subjects or questioners rather than mere objects of curiosity. "Are you a boy or a girl?" can be answered with "I'm a girl. What about you?"

Indeed, Mike Jung's character is devastated when she learns that her background is different from what she thought, because she has lost a key part of her identity and therefore her subjectivity. Furthermore, Chloe can't share what she learns about her family's history with anyone, and she has countless unanswered questions. This was fodder for other conversations with my kids in terms of their experience as transracial adoptees. In our family we talk openly about their respective life histories, because my kids are entitled to know anything and everything they want about their birth families and the circumstances that led to their placement in foster care and eventual adoption into our family.

In Jung's novel, Chloe is not an adoptee, but her parents have cut her off from her history and her heritage through lies and secrecy, which resonates with some of the sad history and problematic discourses around adoption, transracial or not. Some adoptees' parents hide their adoptive status (which I believe, or at least hope, is a rarer occurrence than it once was). There are also systemic injustices within the foster care system, laws that keep adoption records sealed, and manipulation or outright lies that result in adoption against some birth parents' wishes.

Despite Chloe's parents' dishonesty, Jung's novel doesn't paint them as unsympathetic characters, and it's clear that their motivations are good. They want to protect her. They are personally traumatized by the losses they've endured. They are afraid. My children recognized all of this as we read together, but they aligned themselves with Chloe and kept coming back to the unfairness of it all.

"They lied to her," said Stevie. "They lied and lied and lied."

"And now she's supposed to lie, too," said Caroline.

Within these lies are losses for Chloe: loss of trust in her parents, loss of ties to what she'd falsely believed to be her heritage, and loss of stability in her identity. I know that adoption is premised on losses sustained by birth families and adoptees. This is sometimes compounded in transracial adoption when connections between children of color and their respective cultures of origin are severed. As a white person I cannot provide my children with a model of lived experience about what it means to be Black or Latinx or biracial. I read a lot and provide my kids with diverse books and other media, affirm their cultural experiences, provide abundant love for them as their particular selves, and have day-to-day conversations and interactions that support their developing, unique identities.

But my children need other significant people, particularly adult adoptees and people of color, in their lives. And so we live in a diverse neighborhood, they attend diverse public schools (though there are more white, Latinx, and Asian kids than Black students, which hasn't been easy for my Black children), they've all had teachers of color, and our community of friends includes people of color. Two of my daughters participated in a group for adopted teen girls. One of the best resources we've found is the Adoption Mentoring Partnership based at the University of Massachusetts Amherst, through which three of my kids enjoyed college-aged mentors who are also adoptees. Most importantly, they have each other, and all these experiences and relationships provide them with pathways to their future selves, secure in their rightful place in our family and proud of their roots.

My children also know that if they decide one day to try to develop relationships with their birth families, we will support them. Stevie and Caroline and I talked about this as we finished Jung's book, which has an open ending that invites speculation about Chloe's future for learning more about her family's history and perhaps connecting with others. They had empathetic responses for Chloe.

"That would be so happy for her!" said Caroline.

"Is there a sequel so we can see if that really happens? If she learns more about her family and where they come from?" asked Stevie.

"Not yet," I told him, but I hope there will be. In the meantime, I'm grateful that this novel offered me and my kids so much enjoyment *and* opportunity for talking about their lives in the real world.

AUGGIE AND HER, JESS'S DAD AND ME

"Books don't only happen to people. People also happen to books." I love this line from scholar Dr. Louise Rosenblatt so much that I named my blog Book Happenings. *To me, this quotation articulates that a group of people can read the same book, and each person can have a different interpretation and response to it based on their lived experiences. It follows, then, that rereading a book will provoke a different response in the same reader, a notion I explored in this 2016 post for the* Horn Book's Family Reading *blog.*

Katherine Paterson's *Bridge to Terabithia* was one of the first books to make me cry. I was in fourth grade when I read it, and Leslie's death wrecked me. I wept at its suddenness, at the shock that a child died, and at the plain wrongness of it all while my heart ached for Leslie's best friend, Jess. Leslie had seemed like my friend, too, and I felt a sense of solidarity with Jess in his grief.

In fact, rereading this novel as an adult helped me choose "Jesse" as my sixth child's name, and in that reading, Leslie's death and Jess's mourning weren't what made me cry. Instead, I welled up while rereading how Jess's father tries to bridge the gulf that's always separated him from his artistic, sensitive son. I don't recall what I thought about this scene as a child, probably because I didn't think about it very much—at least not with regard to Jess's father. He was an adult, and my focus was on the child characters.

Now I feel a sense of solidarity with Jess's father. He's so familiar to me and so real. His sense of powerlessness as he tries to comfort his son feels palpable now that I'm a mother who's experienced that same helplessness in the face of my own children's pain. There's a rawness to his effort, which is grounded in a familiar desire to erase one's children's suffering, or better yet, protect them from it to begin with.

Of course, we can't protect our children from all hurts, but we can help them navigate loss and pain. Bookish people often grasp at stories as a means of providing comfort and guidance. Offering kids texts that depict a range of human emotion and experience— including grief, loss, tragedy, and death—can be a means of preparing them for the inevitable losses and hurts they'll encounter in an imperfect world. This is one reason that we have an open-bookshelf policy at our house. Kids can read what they wish, and I regularly ask them about their choices. I've found that books can serve as a meeting place for us to talk not just about stories but about their lives, too.

When one of my teenaged daughters was going through a tough time, she came to me and said, "Mom-Mom, this is the first book that ever made me cry."

She was holding R. J. Palacio's *Auggie & Me*. We'd read *Wonder* together with her siblings, and she'd liked it, and she read this companion title independently. She *loved* it.

"What about it made you cry?" I asked her.

"Everything. Just how they all feel their own ways, and how they all have things that can make them sad, because that's *real*."

"Was it hard for you to read all those real feelings in a story?" I asked, thinking about how overwhelming her own emotions had recently been.

"No. I loved it," she said. "It was like they were my friends."

There's a quotation from *Shadowlands*, a biopic about the life of C. S. Lewis, that says, "We read to know we are not alone." I thought of this line when my daughter held the book to her chest, right in front of her own bruised heart.

As my sense of kinship with Jess's dad in *Bridge to Terabithia* reveals, I'm woefully aware of the limits of what I can do to ease my children's hurts. But I took some small comfort in the fact that although Palacio's book wasn't solving problems, it gave my daughter real reassurance that she isn't alone in her emotions.

O, CHRISTMAS BOOKS!

I wrote this piece about Christmas books for the Horn Book *in 2011 as a reflection on how different my children are from each other and from me, too. Memories of shared holiday experiences, including books, bring us together across those differences and give us family stories to tell again and again.*

I was the type of kid who lingered in stairwells trying to over-hear adult conversations and who sneaked downstairs to catch my babysitter making out with her boyfriend. At six, I blew Santa's cover after noticing that his handwriting on gift labels was just like my dad's. My mother was aghast to learn I'd told her friend's daughter (one year my senior) that there was no such thing as Santa Claus. When my mother confronted me, I looked her in the eye and said, "Well, you lied to me!"

When my oldest child, Rory, was a toddler, I wasn't sure I wanted to tell him about Santa at all. "You wouldn't rob him of that!" my mother scolded. *Rob him of what?* I thought. But I knew she meant the wonder of it all, the belief that a magical, benevolent being would grant your wishes. In the end I caved and told Rory the big merry lie; he ate it up like so much gingerbread.

My childhood self scoffed at the idea of flying reindeer, but my son gloried in the magic of beasts that could fly without wings. As a girl I'd noted that even if Santa were to come down our chimney, it was blocked by a woodstove. Rory didn't care that we had no chimney and said Santa would probably come in through the heating vents. I was charmed by his imaginative openness and fed into it, even as I felt a twinge of guilt about lying to my kid. "It's not lying," my mother insisted. "It's about including him in the story."

Picture books played a big part in perpetuating the Santa myth in Rory's life, and we soon amassed a broad library of stories to indulge his fascination. After just a few listens, he flawlessly imitated the British accent of the readers of our audiobook version of Bruce Whatley's *The Night Before Christmas*, and he was baffled by the ending of *The Polar Express*.

"Why can't his sister hear the bell anymore?" he demanded.

"She stopped believing in Santa Claus," I told him. "But the boy kept believing."

"Me, too," said Rory emphatically. "I will always believe."

Rory made good on this promise well into elementary school. He doggedly resisted peer pressure until one autumnal night when he was eight. "Mom-Mom, is Santa real, or do you and Mama put the presents under the tree?"

It was the moment I'd dreaded.

"Why do you ask?" I dodged carefully.

"The other kids say I'm a loser for still believing. Just tell me the truth. I can handle it."

I took a deep breath. "Okay, Rory, Mama and I do put the presents under the tree, but Santa—"

"All of them?" he interrupted as he burst into tears. No, not tears—heaving, racking sobs.

I tried to channel some inner "Yes, Virginia" muse and explained that it's the spirit of Santa that we hold on to—the joy of giving, the celebration of childhood. But Rory would have none of it.

He whispered, "It's like I know the words to the song, but the tune has slipped away."

A knife to the heart, I tell you!

But then he said, "We can't tell Emilia. She still believes."

Yes, his much-younger sister Emilia did believe in Santa, since we included her in the story that her brother loved so well. However, she was terrified of Santa. Just a month or so earlier, Emilia's toddlerhood fascination with babies had led to a love of trains when I read her *New Baby Train*, Marla Frazee's picture-book version of the Woody Guthrie song. She firmly associated babies and trains from then on, doggedly looking for infants in any book about a little engine, including *The Polar Express*. Seeing no babies, Emilia fixated on the jolly old elf—and was struck with horror.

It took me a while to figure out why Emilia suddenly refused to go to bed. Finally, after much prompting, she explained, "If I go to sleep, Santa will come, and Santa is scary!" Emilia had no sense of the passage of time, so telling her that "in a few weeks" Santa would come meant that he could come any minute. She was, after all, the same child who was frightened by masks, clowns, and the potato mascot who ran around our town fair each fall lauding the benefits of fruits and vegetables. It made perfect sense that she would be terrified at the prospect of a big, bearded man prowling around while everyone was asleep. I told her that Santa would leave presents in the garage that year and staged a phone call to the North Pole to tell him not to enter our house.

Later, Caroline, Natayja, and Stevie joined our family in the space of one year. We half-heartedly continued perpetuating the myth, with the thought that if they already had any belief in Santa, it wouldn't be fair to say, "Guess what? In our family he doesn't exist. Happy adoption day!"

Just a few days after Natayja came home to our family, I curled up on the couch with her to read Christmas books.

"Which one do you want?" I asked.

"That one," she said, pointing to Trina Schart Hyman's illustrated edition of Dylan Thomas's *A Child's Christmas in Wales*.

I wasn't sure she'd have the attention span for the long text, but I started reading, "One Christmas was so much like another." We read the book straight through.

This longer story allowed Natayja the uninterrupted time she needed to let her body sink into closeness with mine. Just as the mistletoe hanging in our dining room gave her an excuse to open herself up to kisses, shared reading of this book afforded her the time and space to cuddle. It didn't matter how much she understood, nor that Thomas's Christmas memories were different from her own, nor that in her experience of moving from family to family, one Christmas was so *un*like another. What mattered was the sound of my voice reading to her and the images before her eyes as she pointed to them and said, "Look. It's snowing," or "Firefighters," or "What's that?"

When we reached the end, she asked, "Can we read another one?" It was the first time she'd asked me for anything. We read for more than two hours on that couch, moving from eccentric aunts and candy cigarettes to a train traveling to the North Pole, and yes, to flying reindeer and good old Santa Claus. She delighted in these stories and later in visiting Santa at a local park, where she shyly told him what she wanted him to bring for her and her brothers and sisters and her two new moms.

I'm not sure when or how Natayja discovered that Santa is a story rather than a real person. She's an ideal big sister, protective and kind, and she played along every year for the benefit of her younger siblings. Stevie believed in Santa Claus, but he couldn't hold a Christmas candle to Caroline's devotion, which surpassed even Rory's belief. Caroline read Christmas books all year long, and I indulged her, particularly in her favorite one, another Marla Frazee title, *Santa Claus: The World's Number One Toy Expert*.

"I just love his little underwears!" she said mischievously every time we read it, beholding Santa romping around in his boxers.

But it wasn't just Santa's fashion sense that appealed to her, it was his power. She regarded St. Nick with what seemed like an emphasis on his sainthood, and she worshipped him, perhaps filling some spiritual void in our non-churchgoing household.

Once when Caroline was being bossed around by her siblings, I said, "Ignore them. They're not in charge of the world."

Without missing a beat she responded, "You're right. Santa is."

It seems that Santa, Mrs. Claus, and Rudolph formed Caroline's personal holy trinity as surely as the Father, the Son, and the Holy Ghost formed mine when I was a devout Catholic girl who said her rosary every night, praying to be as good as Mary and delighting in taking part in my church's Christmas pageant. I grew up on Tomie dePaola's pop-up book *The First Christmas*, and it, along with Margaret Wise Brown and Floyd Cooper's *A Child Is Born*, are favorites in my family's library today.

The nativity book we turn to most often, however, is Julie Vivas's *The Nativity*. Vivas's art makes the text—straight from the King James Bible—accessible and wondrously human for her audience. She said of working on this book, "I've been pregnant. I couldn't do a pretty Christmas book." Amen to that! Vivas's pictures of a very pregnant Mary mounting and then riding on a donkey drive this point home with great humor and a subtle feminist panache.

We read this book when Rory was three to prepare for attending Christmas Eve services with my mother. It called for a certain amount of explanation of the text. Vivas's angels wear work boots and have tattered, tie-dyed wings, and Mary is hanging the wash out on the line, oblivious at first to the Archangel Gabriel coming to tell her that she will bear God's child. On the next spread, Mary and Gabriel are seated at the kitchen table, having their important conversation. The expression on Mary's face is one of pure incredulity as she takes in the angel's words: "Fear not Mary: for thou hast found favor with God. Thou shalt bring forth a son and call his name Jesus."

I paraphrased for Rory: "So here the angel is telling Mary that she is going to have a baby, and Mary is really, really surprised about this news. Look at her—she's like, 'Are you kidding?'"

Rory loved this book. We read it dozens of times and brought it to church so he could follow along with the lector. All was well until the "Fear not Mary" line resonated through the quiet sanctuary. Rory, taking this as his cue, called out in full voice, "And Mary was like, *Are you kidding?!*"

I gasped. But my mother whispered, "Oh, Megan, don't worry. Kids are what Christmas is all about," and gave Rory a kiss on the top of his head.

When I think about the story of a long-awaited child born as a symbol of hope, my mother's sentiment is something I want to celebrate in every season, but perhaps especially at Christmastime, with all of its seemingly unavoidable family baggage and chaos. The holiday books I've shared with my kids hold more than stories. They are filled with memories of shared time together. The conversations they've provoked have helped us navigate the emotions that come with being a family composed of people with different dispositions, hopes, and fears. I still question whether I made the right decision in telling my kids about Santa, and I dreaded the day

Caroline would confront me about why the Polar Express hadn't stopped at our house and catch me in the big jolly lie. But I knew that she'd come through it all okay, based on how Rory's feelings evolved over time.

When Rory was twelve, he stayed up after his siblings went to bed to help stuff stockings and wrap presents. He was delighted by his new role and announced, "It's even more fun to *be* Santa than to believe in him." I looked at my son and recalled the night he wept over losing his belief in Santa Claus. Maybe he couldn't hear the bell from the Polar Express, but it seemed that the tune that had slipped away from him was back. Joy to the world, indeed.

THE GIFTS OF A
NOT-SO-WHITE CHRISTMAS

I wrote this post for the EmbraceRace *blog in 2016. I served as a staff blogger during the group's inaugural year, and I've continued to act as a consultant on various projects. The organization's tagline is "Raising a Brave Generation. Together," and its mission is "to raise a generation of children who are thoughtful, informed, and brave about race." It's been such an honor to work with EmbraceRace, and writing this piece was a tribute to a teacher who helped me on the path to anti-racist thinking and action—including in my parenting.*

My husband and I are both lapsed Catholics, and we celebrate Christmas with an emphasis on togetherness, giving gifts, and taking joy in traditions. Although I left the church I grew up in, I still feel a deep connection to many of its stories, the nativity story in particular.

I'm compelled by the birth of a child as an occasion for wonder, hope, celebration, and reverence. I'm grateful for the equation of humble with holy. I'm moved by Joseph embracing his role in Mary and her child's life, despite doubts and misgivings when he learns about her pregnancy. I think of my grandmother's devotion to the Madonna because, as she said, "She was a mother, too," and I regard Mary as a symbol of motherhood that has sustained generations of women in my family.

I can also pinpoint the nativity story as one that helped initiate my serious thinking about race as a young white girl growing up in one of the whitest states in the union, Vermont. From kindergarten through eighth grade, I attended a small independent school that offered French classes starting in first grade. I adored studying French, in part because I was proud of my Franco American heritage and the fact that my father grew up speaking French in his Canadian-border-town-dwelling family.

When my French teacher, Madame Parker, taught my third-grade class a Christmas carol, "Un Flambeau, Jeanette, Isabelle" ("Bring a Torch, Jeanette, Isabella"), my little heart swelled. The song's full lyrics in French and English can be found online. For this story, you need only these four lines:

Look and see how charming is Jesus

How He is white, His cheeks are rosy!

Hush! hush! see how the Child is sleeping;

Hush! hush! see how He smiles in His dreams.

As I read over the mimeographed lyric sheet, I noted that my teacher had crossed out a line (in bold here) and had handwritten words I can no longer recall as a replacement. I asked her why.

"I think the original lyrics are racist," she said plainly.

"Why?" I asked again. "They only say what he looked like."

"But we don't really know what Jesus looked like," she explained. "And we can make a very good guess based on when and where he was born in the Middle East that he was not white-skinned and rosy-cheeked. So saying he was white and rosy as though this is what made him a beautiful baby feels wrong to me." (The first verse calls the baby Jesus beautiful.)

I am, of course, paraphrasing this conversation that happened over thirty years ago, and I'm faithfully reporting what I took away from the brief exchange.

I remember clearly that she used the word "racist." I remember that I objected. I took for granted as truth the representations of the nativity I'd seen in books and in my church. The nativity scene on my grandmother's credenza had one Black wise man among the other human and angelic figurines, who all looked pretty darn white and rosy-cheeked. I was referencing what I knew, or more thoughtfully, what I was *taught*, implicitly or explicitly through artistic and other representations of Jesus and his birth story.

In that third-grade French class, Madame Parker challenged me to rethink what I knew and to reexamine what I took for granted. Although she was intentional in crossing out the line from the song and replacing it, I don't know if she anticipated that anyone would ask her about it. Our exchange had a profound impact on me because a white woman modeled resistance to texts that, intentionally or not, reinforce white supremacy.

It was a way of thinking that set my mind ablaze with possibility. I couldn't have described it like this at the time, but in that class I learned not only French but how to regard all language as something that constructs and is constructed by culture. Within that recognition was an invitation to interrogate what I read as both products and producers of particular worldviews.

I give this gift to my children when I share diverse representations of the nativity story with them. Depicting them only as "white . . . [and] rosy" troubles me. It seems like it not only is a dishonest, ahistorical representation but also equates whiteness with what and whom Christianity regards as holy.

Margaret Wise Brown and Floyd Cooper's *A Child Is Born* was my son Jesse's introduction to the nativity story. After I told him that Christmas celebrates the birthday of a baby named Jesus, he pointed to the Black baby lying in the manger and said, "Baby Jesus happy day-day" (his phrase for happy birthday). Other nativity books on our shelves include depictions of people who appear white in the illustrations (such as Julie Vivas's marvelous feminist *The Nativity*). Like his Black, Latinx, and biracial siblings before him, Jesse, who is white, is growing up with diverse representations of the people in this biblical story.

I extend this commitment to providing my children with diverse representations into secular Christmas stories, too. Christmas books with Black Santas, along with those that represent him as white, are also on our shelves, as are stories about white people,

Native people, Black people, and other people of color celebrating Christmas in contemporary and historical contexts. My children's handmade stockings include knit pictures of a gingerbread man, a snowman, a teddy bear, and a reindeer, and also a white Santa, a Black Santa, and a Black angel. Our tree is decorated with ornaments that hold photos of our multiracial family members over the years and multiracial Santas, angels, elves, and toys.

These diverse representations of the sacred and the secular are a gift my French teacher gave to me when she invited me and my classmates to resist white supremacy. Incidents such as the backlash against the Mall of America's first Black Santa reveal that some people still harbor hateful resistance to anything but a white Christmas. Although I wish there were even more, it's much easier now to find diverse Christmas books, ornaments, and decorations than it was when I first became a mother in 1997. The progress helps my children to regard Christmas as a holiday that belongs to all of them, each and every one.

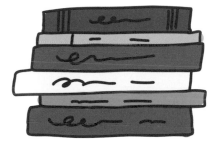

PART
THREE

WINDOW READING WITH
HEY BLACK CHILD

When Reading While White *invited me to write a guest post in 2017, I decided to write about one of my favorite artists, Bryan Collier, and how his work has affected not just my children of color but my white children, too. An important part of book bonding with them involves engaging with stories that decenter whiteness and that encourage them to find common ground with diverse characters.*

When author and editor Andrea Davis Pinkney spoke at the Simmons University Children's Literature Institute one year, she shared one of her go-to sayings as an advocate of diverse children's books: "Show the face." In other words, on book jackets and in picture-book art, illustrations should prominently and regularly show the faces of children of color. Davis's comments immediately brought to mind one of my favorite picture books of 2017, Useni Eugene Perkins and Bryan Collier's *Hey Black Child*. I admire many things about Collier's work, and his dedication to always "show the face" is among them.

The title and text speak directly to the reader and are backed up by jacket art that "shows the face" of two Black children. A boy stands to the left as if anticipating the cover opening up, and a girl stands next to him, her face turned forward, her eyes meeting the reader's. Collier's decision to expand beyond the title's singular "child" and show two children presents an inclusive vision that includes different genders.

And there's more: Turn the book over to look at the back. There's another Black boy and girl, this time with a boy looking at the reader and a bespectacled girl looking to the right. Here Collier introduces the brightly colored balloons that appear throughout the book and add a sense of joy and levity. Rays of light crossing the spine unite the front and back of the jacket and graphically underscore the hopeful, encouraging tone of the book as a whole.

I haven't read this book with my Black children, who are older now. Truth be told, I don't get much opportunity to read picture books with them these days, which is the bittersweet reality of their progress into independent readers. But I *have* read it with one of my younger sons, Jesse, who is white. This book, like others that overtly name race, challenges white readers to resist the colorblind mentality that society teaches. I thought about this as we read *Hey Black Child* and Jesse named his Black brothers and sisters and his Black uncle as people who are or who were Black children like those in Perkins and Collier's book.

The text's repeated refrain, "Hey Black Child," isn't speaking to Jesse, which is an experience I *want* him to have. So much of his world (in children's books and beyond) skews toward privileging him and his experience. Reading this book with Jesse made me recall the *Saturday Night Live* sketch "The Day Beyoncé Turned Black," which aired in 2016 shortly after Beyoncé performed "Formation" at the Super Bowl. In it, white characters are disoriented at best and appalled at worst at the ways that her song centers Blackness.

"Maybe the song isn't for us," exclaims a white man.

"But usually everything is!" cries a white woman in response.

I don't want Jesse to "[lose] his damn white mind" (in the words of the *SNL* sketch) when he comes upon stories or songs that don't center whiteness. Providing him with a rich array of books and media that *don't* imply him as the reader is one step in raising him to resist expecting to find what Dr. Rudine Sims Bishop calls "mirrors" at every turn. He needs "windows," too.

But there are other reasons to share this book with Jesse and with all kids. First is the potential for connections with characters that aren't about race. When we got to the picture of the Black girl suited up for spaceflight, Jesse exclaimed, "I want to be an astronaut like her, too!" He's stated this ambition often, prompting me to find lots of books about space for him. I'm grateful that this picture book's depiction of a Black girl aspiring astronaut is now part of his repertoire of role models, as is *Astronaut Annie* by Suzanne Slade and Nicole Tadgell, *Rocket Says Look Up!* by Nathan Bryon and Dapo Adeola, *Mae Among the Stars* by Roda Ahmed and Stasia Burrington, and *Counting the Stars: The Story of Katherine Johnson, NASA Mathematician* by Lesa Cline-Ransome and Raúl Colón.

I also want *Hey Black Child* in Jesse's hands and in every child's hands simply because it includes the work of one of the most gifted artists of our time. Collier consistently astounds me, particularly with his use of visual metaphor and how it places trust in readers. The sophistication of his work invites children to critically engage with how words and pictures work together to tell stories; convey information; and envision a world in which aspirations, potential, and strengths of all children—especially Black children—are validated and held up to the light.

The stakes are high in our diverse, divided nation, where whiteness is routinely regarded as the norm. Emily Prabhaker, a school-librarian friend of mine, visited a Whole Book Approach course I taught at Simmons University to talk about her use of the model. She told my class about reading a different Collier title—*Trombone Shorty*, an autobiographical picture book by New Orleans musician Troy Andrews—with a majority-white class of sixth graders.

"I know where this book takes place!" said one student as they looked at the jacket art together. "Africa!"

"What do you see that makes you say that?" asked my friend, drawing on Visual Thinking Strategies questions and dreading the "evidence" this student might provide.

"They're all Black," said the student, referencing the group of brown-skinned children on the front and back of the jacket.

I think it's unlikely my white children would look at a book "showing the faces" of a group of Black characters and assume it was set in Africa rather than right here in the United States. Jesse, and now his younger brother, Zachary, have a different lived experience than my friend's students. And yet they are still immersed in a society in which white is defined as the norm, and they aren't immune to that messaging. That's why reading "window" books with them is such an important part of our book bonding.

DAVE THE POTTER
AND STEVIE THE READER

An illustration from Dave the Potter: Artist, Poet, Slave *by Laban Carrick Hill and Bryan Collier hangs in my living room. In it, Dave stands in front of a tree with his arms outstretched like the branches behind him. His eyes are closed as he tilts his face upward, and if you look closely, you can see faces collaged into the tree branches. I interpret the tree as a symbol of Dave's heritage, a family tree reaching back into his ancestry and acknowledging, perhaps, the family from which he was separated. I purchased the print as a memento of my Caldecott Award Selection Committee service, and I also wanted it in our home in honor of my Black children's heritage. It's a book that played a key role in one son's racial-identity development, which is the focus of this 2011 piece from the* Horn Book Magazine.

One of the things I love best about my work in children's literature is how seamlessly it melds with my life as a mother. When I was selected to serve on the 2011 Caldecott Award committee, I wrote to family and friends, saying, "Thousands of picture books will come my way, and I have the perfect test audience waiting at home. It's all feeling pretty happily ever after." I'd overestimated the number of books I would receive (close to seven hundred), but I was right to anticipate how well my committee service would dovetail with mothering. Every new box of books delivered to my door was a source of pleasure for me and my children as we eagerly dove in to see what stories and art awaited us.

One of the books our committee chose to honor was *Dave the Potter: Artist, Poet, Slave* by Laban Carrick Hill and Bryan Collier. I think of this book as a meditation on the triumph of the human spirit and artistic expression in the face of oppression, and it offers poetic text, enriching information, and downright gorgeous and emotionally powerful illustrations.

Although my older children looked at it, and I used it with great success in mock Caldecott sessions I led with a local sixth-grade class, it wasn't a book I read with my younger children at home. In retrospect, I think I shied away from it as read-aloud fare for then four- and five-year-old Caroline and Stevie, thinking that they didn't yet have the historical knowledge or maturity to grapple with the reality of Dave's life as an enslaved person. Eventually I decided that I wanted to read all three of the books our Caldecott committee selected with all of my kids in order to share the experience with them.

Medal winner *A Sick Day for Amos McGee* by Philip C. Stead and Erin E. Stead, and Honor book *Interrupting Chicken* by David Ezra Stein were titles that my kids already knew and loved. As I picked up *Dave the Potter* to read aloud one night, I reckoned with my whiteness and how it contributed to the fact that I'd neglected to share this book with my youngest children. Ultimately, Caroline wasn't particularly invested. But I witnessed Stevie's enthrallment with the story and art, and I rediscovered the book as a brilliant introduction to some of the hard truths of American history rather than one that demands broad historical context or sophistication.

I've often found myself striving to shelter my Black children from the painful impact of historical and contemporary racism while instilling in them a sense of pride in their heritage and preparing them to resist oppression and prejudice. I haven't personally been targeted by anti-Black racism, so the best I can do is act as an ally. This is something I've held on to as I've read books like *Dave the Potter* with them, explaining that people with skin like mine enslaved people with skin like theirs, while also acknowledging that as children of Puerto Rican, Jamaican, African American, Irish, and Franco American heritage, they have individual biological family histories that align and depart from any particular history in different ways. It's complicated!

"It is so amazing that Dave learned how to read and write," I told my kids as we looked at the closing picture of him etching a poem into the side of one of his pots.

"Why?" Stevie asked. "He's a grown-up."

"Remember how we talked about what the word *slave* in the title means?" I asked. Stevie nodded, as did Natayja sitting behind him, and then Emilia piped up: "It means you're not free. And it's really bad because that means people owned other people."

"Yes," I said, watching Stevie's face as he absorbed all this. "Because way back then, when white people enslaved Black people in this country, they also made laws to keep Black people from learning how to read or write because that could make them more powerful."

"That's not fair," Stevie said.

"No, it's not. None of it was fair. But Dave learned how to read and write anyway, and he learned how to make these pots. He was very smart and very brave."

"I'm learning how to read and write now, too," Stevie said proudly. I felt him forging a connection between himself as an African American boy beginning to grapple with racism and Dave as an enslaved Black man asserting his dignity and worth in a society that railed against it.

"Read *all* of Dave's poems," Stevie insisted when we reached the back matter of the book, which includes the words that Dave wrote on his pots. And so I did.

I doubt Stevie grasped the meaning of every short poem, but I know he was moved by the power of the story of this man's life and art.

"Let me see that book again," he said, reaching for it.

And for the next twenty minutes or so, I tried to give him space for a private communion with the book, as the girls and I shifted gears and read from Natalie Babbitt's *The Search for Delicious.* I couldn't resist stealing glimpses of Stevie as he traced his fingers around the edges of the pots in the illustrations and studied Dave's face from page to page.

Although we keep most of our children's books on the built-in bookcases of the room we call the "children's library" at home, Stevie brought *Dave the Potter* to his bedroom that night. I've since read it with him and seen him looking at it by himself many times. One night, he said, "It isn't nice to make people work and not pay them." Later he asked, "Why didn't they run away?"

"Some people did," I told him, and then we talked about Harriet Tubman and the Underground Railroad as I made a mental note to share some of the many books we own about that part of American history. Emilia was already familiar with Tubman's name, and she said that Tubman was very brave for helping so many people escape to freedom.

"So did she get everybody except for Dave?" Stevie asked, his face falling as he thought about this particular person, one of myriad enslaved people in his new knowledge of American history.

"No, she didn't get everybody. There were too many people to help. But she helped lots and lots of people," I told him.

We talked about how enslaved people made lives for themselves in defiance of a system that denied their humanity. I told them that this was a source of pride for many. Stevie beamed as we talked about bravery, hope, and rebellion, and I know how deeply he felt the injustice of it all. As I reflect on this awakening in my little boy, one step in many he took from innocence to experience, I am grateful for books and the discussions that they've provoked. They've played a crucial role in helping me mother my children as they grow up and discover where they came from, who they are, and who they might yet become. Of course I want to protect Stevie, and I ached as I watched him try to wrap his mind around the idea that a person could own another person. I was also deeply moved by his reaction to this book's affirmation of Dave's triumph and by his proud sense of identification with it.

"He has dark-brown skin like me because we are both African American," Stevie said as he looked at *Dave* for the umpteenth time. I recalled his earlier fascination with the differences in skin color that exist in our multiracial, adoptive family and in the broader world around him.

"I know how I got this dark-brown skin," he told me when he was three years old.

"How?" I asked, wondering if he would talk about his birth parents.

"Well. When I was borned, I just got to choose, and I choosed this dark-brown skin because I thought it was the most beautiful."

"Like *Beautiful Blackbird*?" I asked him, referencing Ashley Bryan's picture book.

"Uh-huh!" Stevie quoted. Then he quickly added, "But I am not really the color black. I am dark, dark brown."

Later, when he was anticipating the start of kindergarten, he asked me, "Does my teacher know I have brown skin?"

"I don't know," I told him. "Why?"

"I just wondered," he said, very matter-of-factly. "And does she have skin like me, or you, or in the middle like Emilia?"

"I don't know," I said again, and I reflected on the erroneous goal some adults have of raising colorblind children. Was Stevie, being raised by white parents, hoping he would have a Black teacher as caregiver and role model? Were his questions about skin color really innocent of the value society places on racial constructions? I couldn't be sure, but I doubted it, and that's all the more reason why I'm dedicated to the discussions we have at home about race, skin color, racism, oppression, and resistance. I have always hoped that they play a role in contributing to Stevie's positive self-concept.

Meanwhile, I know that other factors are at play, too, including the inner, core, emotional resilience that Stevie displays. Acknowledging strengths is something I try to do in my parenting in an effort to avoid misguided, overprotective impulses regarding my children's individual forays—intellectual and otherwise—into the deeply flawed but beautiful world they've inherited. Sometimes, as in my not-so-well-thought-out failure to read *Dave the Potter* to Stevie before it won a Caldecott Honor, I fall short. I underestimate my children's resilience and capacity for reading and thinking about complex and difficult issues.

Of course, I'm not alone in the struggle to balance honesty with protective impulses. A few years ago, the Eric Carle Museum of Picture Book Art hosted an exhibition of illustrations from Julius Lester and Jerry Pinkney's *The Old African*. Curators decided to place small signs outside the gallery to warn visitors with young children about the graphic nature of pictures depicting the Middle Passage and other scenes in which enslaved people are tied and beaten. The impulse was not censorious but intended to provide a heads-up that the images would likely demand contextual conversations. Some pictures are worth well over a thousand words.

I worked at the Carle at the time, and I know that some people did not see the signs and were caught unaware when they walked into the gallery with their young children. Others had only cursory conversations about the pictures. They didn't seem to know how to talk with their children about such horrors. But many parents and teachers who spoke with me about the exhibition were grateful for its content and for the rich, if difficult, conversations it elicited.

"It's not like there *should* be a pretty, gentle book about slavery," one mother said to me.

And I couldn't agree more. *Dave the Potter* does not present as harrowing a depiction of slavery as *The Old African* or Tom Feelings's *Middle Passage*. At the same time, it is not gentle, since it doesn't flinch from the reality of Dave's bondage even as it depicts his expressions of resistance against it. My readings of Eloise Greenfield's poem "Harriet Tubman" from *Honey, I Love and Other Love Poems* and Ellen Levine and Kadir Nelson's *Henry's Freedom Box* with my children proved inspirational and enriching in their own right, but I value the fact that *Dave the Potter* is a book about a person who did *not* escape slavery—because, as Stevie learned, so many did not.

It's heartbreaking to talk with children about slavery and about other times and ways—in the past and now—that humans have behaved inhumanely toward fellow humans. Perhaps it's more complicated in families like mine. But to avoid such conversations or to address them in ways that minimize their tragedy is to engage not in heartbreak but in heartshrink.

Reading with my children has shown me that books like *Dave the Potter* can enrich their visions of the complex world while also preparing them to, in time, write their own chapters in history, as surely as Dave penned his.

ADRIAN SIMCOX IS NOT A MOCKINGBIRD (OR, EMPATHY FOR CRITICAL READERS)

Most of this piece originated as a post for the Horn Book's *2018* Calling Caldecott *blog, where (after some careful reflection) I was delighted to support Marcy Campbell and Corinna Luyken's* Adrian Simcox Does NOT Have a Horse. *I've expanded that post to include how talking with my son about his eighth-grade class reading of Harper Lee's* To Kill a Mockingbird *served as a backdrop for my thinking about this picture book.*

My son Stevie's response to Harper Lee's *To Kill a Mockingbird* when he read it in his eighth-grade English class was akin to that of writer and scholar Dr. Roxane Gay, who wrote in the *New York Times* in 2018, "Perhaps I am ambivalent because I am black. I am not the target audience. I don't need to read about a young white girl understanding the perniciousness of racism to actually understand the perniciousness of racism. I have ample first-hand experience."

Stevie was aghast at his white classmates' naivete. "They're just like Jem!" he said incredulously, referencing protagonist Scout's older brother. "How could they be surprised that Tom Robinson [a Black man falsely accused of raping a white woman] gets convicted?"

He went on to rail against the text and (among other things) asserted a powerful critique about its ahistorical scene when three white children, Scout, Dill, and Jem, turn back a lynch mob.

"That's not realistic!" he said. "I mean, if it was that easy, then maybe all those Black people wouldn't have been killed."

Stevie and I talked about how the scene provides a white savior, which creates wish fulfillment for white readers. Hey, look at these white kids doing the right thing, and look at those white grown-ups changing. But the dishonesty at the heart of the scene is dismaying at best to a reader like my son. It offers him the opposite of empathy, as it roundly dismisses his understanding of the history of lynching in the United States.

"Why do people talk about this book like it's all about being against racism?" Stevie said during another conversation. "It's not even really about the Black people in the story. It's about all the white people."

He had a point. A former graduate student of mine, Autumn Allen, wrote in the journal *Research on Diversity in Youth Literature* in 2020 about an oft-quoted line from Scout's father, Atticus Finch: "You never really understand a person until you consider things from his point of view . . . until you climb into his skin and walk around in it." She pointed out that the line is not aimed at getting Scout and Jem to empathize with Black people like Tom Robinson; his wife, Helen; and the Finch family's maid, Calpurnia. No, Autumn clarified, Atticus means that the children should try to understand Boo Radley, who is ostracized but not persecuted, and who is white. This is just one way that Black characters are marginalized and silenced in this book, so they end up serving as vehicles for white characters' (incremental) growth.

Stevie's teacher, Michael Lawrence-Riddell, was a white, progressive man who went on to establish an outstanding resource for American history educators, Self-Evident Education. He did an admirable job of centering Black stories and history as context for teaching Lee's novel. I supplemented Stevie's study with books at home about Ida B. Wells and Black-led anti-lynching activism, including *Ida B. Wells-Barnett: Strike a Blow Against a Glaring Evil* by Anne Schraff. Nevertheless, my son had a consistent feeling of frustration and pain throughout the unit.

It was against this backdrop that I first heard of Marcy Campbell's debut picture book, *Adrian Simcox Does NOT Have a Horse,* illustrated by Corinna Luyken, in which the protagonist is bullied because of his poverty. Before reading it, I encountered several reviews that likened it to Eleanor Estes's classic chapter book *The Hundred Dresses*. Just as many readers regard *To Kill a Mockingbird* as an anti-racist text, many describe *The Hundred Dresses* as a book that fosters empathy for poor people. But I can't shake my own reading of the bullied, impoverished victim, Wanda Petronski. To me, she is a pitiable vehicle through which the narrator, Maddie (a bystander to the bullying), achieves growth. I'm mighty tired of narratives that offer up a suffering marginalized person so another character can ever-so-slowly awaken to their pain, so I was leery of *Adrian Simcox*. Would this picture book undermine its ostensible aim of fostering empathy by marginalizing the bullied, lower-class Adrian Simcox, as surely as my son and I feel that *Mockingbird* marginalizes its Black characters and *Dresses* does the same to Wanda Petronski?

No. Through their sensitive depiction of Adrian Simcox and his imaginary horse, author Marcy Campbell and particularly artist Corinna Luyken prevent material poverty from indicating an innate purity that helps a tormentor see the error of her cruel ways. It does so by focusing on Adrian's magnificent imagination instead of Chloe-the-bully's (eventual) growth. The result is that readers are visually invited to align themselves with Adrian and his horse— and not with Chloe and her judgments.

Jacket art immediately prompts an allegiance between the reader and Adrian. Chloe and Adrian stand on either side of the title, the words stacked like a wall between them. Chloe has her back to the far-right edge of the cover, and Adrian faces her. The reader must go against Chloe's stance in order to open the book, lifting the cover even though she has her back to it. And there is a white, decidedly equine shape that evokes a horse. We begin the book able to see the horse that Chloe claims Adrian doesn't have.

Several interior spreads reward the reader with I-spy delight in repeated appearances of Adrian's horse, served up as powerful visual counterpoints to Chloe's persistent denial of its existence. However, the emotional climax of the story, in which Chloe confronts Adrian, does not feature any horse imagery, hidden or otherwise. A close-up of Chloe's profile fills the left side of the spread, and Adrian's fills the right. They are separated, and the white of the page forces the reader to see only them. The isolation of the text on Chloe's side underscores Adrian's vulnerable silence as he waits to see if she will again hurl accusations at him.

Happily, the better angels of Chloe's disposition rise up in the next pages, and she no longer torments Adrian. The penultimate spread bursts with golden color, and Adrian is large and strong, his head bowed and eyes closed. The large, vertical swath of open space creates his horse's profile, leaning down as though to nuzzle him. Can Chloe finally see his horse? The accompanying text reads, "And then I thought Adrian Simcox had just about the best imagination of any kid in our whole school." This suggests that by finally, truly listening to Adrian, Chloe begins to at least, and at last, see *him*.

The concluding spread affirms that, yes, she sees his horse, too. It's more distinct here—its head and neck arching protectively over Adrian and its tail toward Chloe—"the most beautiful horse of anyone, anywhere." The grass Chloe holds even helps form the horse's body by outlining its rear flanks. Chloe's expression is now wondrous, and Adrian is relaxed and engaged.

This picture book can certainly provoke reflections on class and kindness. But its achievement shines brightest in how Luyken's illustrations complicate the book's call for empathy. Luyken asks readers to regard Adrian not as a poor victim but as something of a hero. Meanwhile, Chloe's poverty of imagination is to be pitied, as artistic invitations ask readers to align themselves with Adrian instead.

So how does this all connect back to Stevie's experience with *To Kill a Mockingbird*? As a novel without illustrations, it doesn't have the opportunity to complicate the text that's focused on white characters with visual art that centers the Black characters and their experiences. And Stevie couldn't find a way to embrace the text as anti-racist when, in his reading, it marginalizes Black characters. He therefore read it while resisting, feeling isolated in his class as he did so.

In the comment stream of the original online version of this essay, a teacher quoted Atticus Finch's line about walking around in another person's skin in praise of how *Adrian Simcox Does NOT Have a Horse* fosters empathy. I replied that I was working on an expanded version of the essay, including Lee's novel and how I co-read it with my Black son. I linked to a #DisruptTexts Twitter thread from educator Tricia Ebarvia about the novel. Well, let's just say the teacher wasn't interested. He posted a total of ten times in defense of Lee's novel even though no one responded to him. I found it quite ironic, and sad, really, that I'd tried to tell him what my son and I and many others see in Lee's novel, only to have him act like Chloe in Campbell and Luyken's picture book.

Thankfully this was not the case at my son's middle school, where the English department decided to remove *To Kill a Mockingbird* from its curriculum. The department head approached me for recommendations that could be used to enrich a curricular focus on social justice. They'd already been discussing titles like John Lewis, Andrew Aydin, and Nate Powell's *March* trilogy; Angie Thomas's *The Hate U Give*; Nic Stone's *Dear Martin; All American Boys* by Jason Reynolds and Brendan Kiely; *The 57 Bus* by Dashka Slater; and *Love, Hate & Other Filters* by Samira Ahmed. To this excellent list, I added other suggestions; some I knew Stevie had read, and others I wished he would so I could talk with him about them. (See the list at the back of this book.)

Prioritizing books by and about Black people, Indigenous people, and other people of color in a curriculum is an essential first step in enacting anti-racist pedagogy. Doing so has the potential to not just uplift students of color but to transform white students' learning by encouraging them toward true empathy. But only assigning books isn't enough. The year after Stevie's experience with *To Kill a Mockingbird*, his English class read Lorraine Hansberry's play *A Raisin in the Sun*. While he appreciated the play itself, and its title's connection to Langston Hughes's poem "Harlem," Stevie shared that it was uncomfortable to sit in a majority-white classroom listening to his classmates read the play aloud in what he termed "Black southern dialects."

"That's awful," I told him. "You deserve to learn in your classroom, and how can you learn if you're feeling so uncomfortable or if you're distracted from the text by other people's readings?"

"I was just venting," he told me. "Don't go and email my teacher or do anything crazy!"

I promised Stevie I would be measured in the email I felt I had to write. "I'm a teacher, too," I told him. "And if one of my students was feeling this way, I would want to know."

Stevie's teacher responded with compassion, and he immediately reinforced with the class that they were in no way to mock or enact caricatures of the dialogue as they read aloud.

"Is it any better?" I asked Stevie after hearing about this turn of events.

"Yeah," he said. "And he was really cool about it. He didn't say anything about me or your email or anything."

The relief in my son's voice was palpable, and I was relieved, too, since I'd taken a risk in going against Stevie's wishes. Critical literacy asserts that when we read a book, we read the world because a text is a reflection of its time and place, and we read in the context of our lived experience. My son, and all students, need and deserve to see their realities reflected back to them in literature and to have the contexts in which they read be seen and honored, too. Stevie's teacher recognized that, which enabled my son to build trust in him and therefore to learn better overall.

ALONGSIDE, NOT DESPITE: TALKING ABOUT RACE AND SETTLER COLONIALISM IN CHILDREN'S LITERATURE

I wrote this essay in 2017—my first post for Reading While White. *It reveals how much my thinking about the Little House on the Prairie series has changed over time. At what cost do we hold on to books we read as children that we now find objectionable? How might our book bonding with our children decolonize children's literature instead of reinforcing biases? It's taken me too long to get to these questions, but I am asking now, and I think my children's (reading) lives are better for it.*

For several years, I taught a graduate course called The Child and the Book at Simmons University. We critically examined how children, childhood, reading, and childhood reading are represented in fiction. We started with Dr. Rudine Sims Bishop's "Mirrors, Windows, and Sliding Glass Doors" framework to consider who is included and who is excluded in discourse about childhood and reading. The class read adult memoirs about childhood reading, and we addressed adults' roles in children's reading experiences. I opened the semester with an assignment that asked students to revisit a book from their childhood in order to juxtapose their memories of reading it with their reactions while rereading as adults. This exercise highlights the slipperiness of memory, the pitfalls of sentimentality and nostalgia, and the instability of meaning over time.

The majority of my students were white women, and almost every time I gave this assignment, I had students revisit a book from Laura Ingalls Wilder's Little House on the Prairie series. I also used to assign either *Little House in the Big Woods* or *Little House on the Prairie* in this course, and we inevitably examined the Little House series' overt racism and the unvarnished idealization of settler colonialism and westward expansion. Once I paused the discussion after a student said she was struggling with how to reconcile her fond childhood memories of co-reading the books with her mother and her contemporary recognition of how the series perpetuates abhorrent ideologies.

"I feel bad saying I love these books despite their racism," she said.

"Then don't say that," I told her. "Say you love them alongside their racism, and then interrogate what that means for you as a white reader."

I don't think this made her feel less "bad," but that wasn't my goal. Some of the best learning happens when students are uncomfortable. To quote scholars Dr. Perry Nodelman and Dr. Mavis Reimer in *The Pleasures of Children's Literature*: "Although certainty is comfortable, it can also be oppressive and limiting."

An important part of my role as a teacher is to prevent discomfort from devolving into defensiveness. My suggestion to say "alongside" rather than "despite" was spontaneous that day, but it ended up being an effective tool to push students beyond affective, nostalgic responses and into critical engagement. The word *despite* would've allowed white students to neatly avoid confronting the racism, clinging to a reading imbued with a false racial innocence. On the other hand, the word *alongside* prompted white students to grapple with the racial privilege necessary to say they loved a book even as they plainly saw its racism. They progressed toward considering how they might respond to a similar statement about a book that denigrated a group to which they belong: "I love this book alongside its misogyny, its anti-Semitism, its Islamophobia, its homophobia, its ableism, its classism . . ."

Many of my students were future teachers and librarians, so we considered how actions, not just words, can communicate attitudes toward particular books through decisions about displays, book talks, programming, curriculum, or collection development. During a discussion, a student asked, "But how can we know which books will harm or offend which readers, patrons, or students?"

I am not a librarian, nor am I a classroom teacher. But for nearly a decade I worked at the Eric Carle Museum of Picture Book Art, where I led drop-in storytimes and oversaw the reading library. Whenever I get the chance to lead a storytime as a volunteer there, or in my kids' classrooms or as a visiting author with picture books of my own, I'm careful to always include books by diverse authors and illustrators. I also track the titles I use with a diversity and inclusion audit in order to keep myself accountable (a practice I advocated to my students and modeled in my syllabi).

These days, the young readers I interact with most often are my own children, and issues of representation, diversity, and inclusion are every bit as important in my family reading life as they have been in my professional life. My oldest son might scoff at what he reads as a flat, racist caricature of a Black teenager devoid of humanity and brush it away like so much dirt off his shoulder. My other Black son might feel personally wounded and wonder, "Is this how other people see me?" *Both* are harmed and endangered, however, by the perpetuation of dehumanizing depictions of Black people in a society rife with the stereotype of the Black male menace to society.

While I believe that the potential for individual harm is important, it isn't the only factor when I—and, I'd wager, other people—speak out about racism in books for young people, guide students to consider how critical reading informs work with children's literature, or purchase or borrow books for reading at home. I also think about how literature, like any art, not only reflects culture and sociopolitical power structures but helps create them.

The stakes are high when the words *Black Lives Matter* are still routinely met with resistance. Indigenous scholar Dr. Debbie Reese (Nambé Pueblo), often writes on her blog about how Native people are routinely relegated to the past and erased as contemporary members of sovereign nations. I'm not saying that calling out racism and idealized depictions of settler colonialism in children's books will prevent violent racism and attacks on Black people or Native people and Native sovereignty. I am saying that the stories we tell (and read and teach and display and circulate) can subvert or reinforce underlying thoughts and beliefs about race and white supremacy. And those contribute to violence and often allow perpetrators to act without consequence.

Critiquing books that reinforce such ideologies can feel as if it's not useful enough. But seeing my students push their critical thinking about books and the child readers they work with gave me hope. There's grace in this work, and it's necessary when creating and advocating for diverse books that can help create a safer, more humane society.

So how does this relate to reading with my family or to my work with students? Note that above I said that I *used to* assign a book from the Little House on the Prairie series. I don't anymore. Instead, I engage in what critical race theory calls counter-storytelling by assigning books like *The Birchbark House* by Louise Erdrich (Turtle Mountain Chippewa). It's a book that centers Indigenous stories and history, and I leave out books like Wilder's that present the dominant narrative of settler colonialism. Our culture has made sure that my students already know that narrative.

At home, I made the same shift. Years ago, I read my childhood copy of *Little House in the Big Woods* with a few of my older children in an attempt to engage them in a resistant reading about a false history of empty land settled by brave, white pioneers. Because of prior conversations and readings at home and at school, they pretty much took that reading for granted. ("Yes, we already know Columbus didn't discover America, the Thanksgiving story is a lie, and there were plenty of Native people living in the big woods, so the Ingalls basically stole that land.") Instead, they were fascinated by the religiosity of the text, contrasting it with their secular lives. My initial takeaway was that I should trust them as critical readers, and I should back off. I didn't read later books in the series with my kids because my rereadings had me slack-jawed at just how overtly, unapologetically racist they are. I didn't want my children to engage with those books, even to interrogate them. (As an aside, I often wonder if people who defend the Little House on the Prairie books or myriad other texts critiqued as racist have reread them as adults, or if their defense is based on decades-old childhood readings.)

I also haven't read *Little House in the Big Woods* with my youngest children, who are white, even to point out its flaws. I do see tremendous value in lining our bookshelves with books by and about Indigenous people. Erdrich's Birchbark House series is there, and so too are novels like *Indian Shoes* by Cynthia Leitich Smith (Muscogee) and *How I Became a Ghost* by Tim Tingle (Choctaw), alongside nonfiction like *Speaking Our Truth: A Journey of*

Reconciliation by Monique Gray Smith (Cree, Lakota) and *We Are Grateful: Otsaliheliga* and *We Are Still Here! Native American Truths Everyone Should Know* by Traci Sorell (Cherokee), and picture books and board books like *Birdsong* by Julie Flett (Cree-Métis), *At the Mountain's Base* by Traci Sorell and Weshoyot Alvitre (Tongva/Scots-Gaelic), and *Little You* and *We Sang You Home* by Richard Van Camp (Dogrib Tłįchǫ). Most of these books are about contemporary Indigenous people, and by virtue of their existence, they resist that harmful myth of the vanished Indian asserted by the first lines of *Little House in the Big Woods* and reinforced by other romanticized depictions of westward expansion.

I want my children to know that there are over five hundred diverse, sovereign Native nations in what we call the United States. They should learn this not despite their reading but because of it. I still trust my kids to be critical readers, but becoming so isn't a passive process, and I recognize my responsibility to help them toward this goal.

READING *LAST STOP ON MARKET STREET* AND OTHER DIVERSE BOOKS *WITH* CHILDREN

This essay first appeared in 2016 in the Horn Book Magazine. *I'd seen firsthand how Caldecott Honor and Newbery Medal winner* Last Stop on Market Street *by Matt de la Peña and Christian Robinson sparked meaningful conversations with children about empathy and inclusivity. The year the book won its awards, I'd heard a false dichotomy of "quality vs. diversity." I wrote this piece to push back against those discomfited by the historically diverse and inclusive ALA Youth Media Award winners that year. It's just one of many books I recommend for fostering book bonding in service of social justice.*

Like Christian Robinson's Caldecott Honor–winning artwork, Matt de la Peña's Newbery Medal–winning writing is deceptively simple and gloriously layered in *Last Stop on Market Street*. In my initial readings, one line stood out to me: "They sat right up front." Although it denotes where on the bus CJ and Nana sit down, it also connotes layers of history. I brought this point up with my children when we read the book together at home.

"Nana is African American," I began. "So when she was a little girl, if she rode a bus with *her* nana it might have been illegal for them to sit 'right up front.'"

My oldest son, Rory, was home from college on his winter break, and I'd managed to gather all my kids in the living room for an incredibly rare all-family storytime. The baby was most interested in climbing from one lap to another, but the other kids were engaged, and after my comment about segregation, they brought up Rosa Parks and wondered what Nana's name was.

"Maybe it's Rosa?" my daughter Caroline said.

Well, Nana is forever Rosa to me now.

When we reached the page where Nana greets the blind man who compliments her perfume, I read, "Nana squeezed the man's hand and laughed her deep laugh." I paused for my kids' responses to the scene, expecting some commentary about the primary characters' interactions.

Instead, my daughter Emilia said, "That person's a creeper!"

I scanned the spread and homed in on the tattooed, bald man wearing a white tank top.

Oh dear, I thought. *We should unpack this.* How could I validate my daughter's inclination to go with her gut but not get carried away with judgments? I resorted to the trustiest tool in my toolbox: open-ended questions.

"What do you see that makes you say that?" I asked.

"Look at her! She's totally looking at that guy's phone. And she was on the other page, too!" Emilia said, incredulous. She meant the superbly specific "old woman with curlers [who] had butterflies in a jar."

"Yeah!" said Stevie. "She's a total creeper!" Much laughter ensued.

Oops. *I'd* been the one making assumptions based on appearance. Emilia, and in her footsteps, Stevie, made a judgment on firmer ground: someone's actions.

Our reading went on. We talked about how CJ reminded them of Ezra Jack Keats's Peter from *The Snowy Day* on the spread when CJ closes his eyes and listens to music, and how the title of this book is a line in the story.

"It's like *Where the Wild Things Are*," I offered. "The title makes you focus on the place where the characters go."

This connection prompted my kids to reflect on how good it is that CJ and Nana help others at a soup kitchen, thus fulfilling my intent that our reading would consider the artful way the text invites readers to engage in historical and social commentary. Emilia's "that person's a creeper" comment stuck with me. Her words reminded me anew that meaning resides in the spaces between a reader and art and text. In other words, we can all arrive at different conclusions, emphases, and interpretations about and from a book based on our own frameworks.

Children's literature exists at a tricky remove from its audience. Adults write, illustrate, and often select and read books aloud to children. This affords adults a great deal of power—including imposing our own interpretations instead of inviting children to voice theirs. When I lead children's storytimes, I endeavor to make children's questions and responses as integral as the book itself. My own book *Reading Picture Books with Children: How to Shake Up Storytime and Get Kids Talking About What They See* details my Whole Book Approach storytime model, which I developed in association with the Eric Carle Museum of Picture Book Art. Using that model, I read *Last Stop on Market Street* to a kindergarten class.

One thing I like to do is point out different book design and production elements and ask kids what they notice about them. In this book, I showed the children the endpapers and said, "Endpapers often give us clues, so let's take a look to see what's here, and then remember what we talked about as we read the story."

The children noticed that the endpapers were bright yellow, like the sweater that CJ wears on the cover, and then they started listing the things they saw in the endpapers' pictures.

"A bus like on the cover!"

"A guitar."

"A dog."

"An umbrella."

"A fancy money." (A phrase from a child searching for the word *coin* or *quarter*.)

And so on.

On the title page, the children recognized the boy and the woman from the jacket and guessed that she was his grandma.

"What do you see that makes you say that?" I asked.

"She is old with white hair," one kid offered.

"Yes, but that's not her cane," said another child. "That's the umbrella we saw, all folded up."

It was working. Kids were seeing how the whole book—all the parts of the book—work together to construct character and tell the story.

The group was quiet as I read the text aloud, and I watched for their reactions to the story and the illustrations. When we reached the spread depicting the bus pulling up, I read Nana's words, "Boy, what do we need a car for? We got a bus that breathes fire."

A child interjected, "Because of the dragon."

The dragon? I wondered. I'd thought Nana was referring to the bus expelling exhaust. Prompted by this child, I looked more closely and saw a fire-breathing dragon on the side of the bus.

I am not a strong visual thinker. I have to work hard to read illustrations, and oftentimes I see things only after kids point them out to me. That's one of the reasons that using the Whole Book Approach and slowing down to really talk about art and design is so rewarding. This particular interaction about the fire-breathing bus made me take a moment to think through how to get kids to examine the interdependence of art and text in other spreads.

One page reads, "Two older boys got on next. CJ watched as they moved on by and stood in the back. 'Sure wish I had one of those,' he said."

I paused and asked the children, "What does CJ wish he had?" This was intended to invite them to read the picture and interpret its interaction with the ambiguous text.

"A big brother," said one kindergartner without missing a beat, and my heart melted. Here was a child who seemed like a pint-sized Nana in his outlook on life. He was, as my mother might say, "an old soul."

I smiled at him and said, "He *is* looking up at those boys, isn't he?" and then I asked the group, "What else might CJ be wishing for?"

"A dog!" was the next response.

This was certainly an anti-materialistic group of kindergartners.

I read on. "Nana set down her knitting. 'What for? You got the real live thing sitting across from you. Why don't you ask that man if he'll play you a song?'"

"Oh!" said one of the kindergartners. "He was wishing for that boy's phone to listen to music."

I invited the children to close their eyes along with the blind man, Nana, CJ, and the spotted dog. Then I said, "Now open them," so they could see how Robinson's art makes music visible on one ebullient spread. They were riveted. And as I looked at them taking in the art and hearing the words read aloud, I wondered what each child was thinking. They didn't offer up any comments, and sensing something sacred in the air, I decided not to prompt them. What I'm sure of is that all of them had thoughts and feelings and ideas in response to Robinson's art and de la Peña's text.

Although most of the trainings I do about reading with children are for teachers and librarians, I've had increasing opportunities to work with parent groups, too. Often parents want to use picture books to facilitate conversations with children about difficult topics or to affirm and empower them in the face of oppression and fear. For example, I led a KidLit Marches for Kids contingent as part of the widespread 2018 March For Our Lives spearheaded by youth activists in the wake of the deadly school shooting at Marjory Stoneman Douglas High School in Parkland, Florida. Then I led a family storytime featuring *We March* by Shane W. Evans, *You Hold Me Up* by Monique Gray Smith and Danielle Daniel, and *Why Am I Me?* by Paige Britt, Selina Alko, and Sean Qualls. I included these books on a longer list of titles recommended to spark conversations with children about empathy, kindness, and youth activism. (See the list at the back of this book.) Families who attended voiced despair over how to keep their children safe—from gun violence and also from fear. "We need to feel like we are doing *something*," a mother said to me. "This helps."

That experience led a group called We Stand Together to contact me in the wake of the massacre of eleven people at the Tree of Life Synagogue in Pittsburgh in October 2018. They were leading what they called a "Hannukah Ally Action." People could print out a picture of a menorah and hang it in a window of their home to show pride in their Jewish heritage or solidarity with Jewish people. The organizers wanted to host a family event that would provide a sense of community and promote healing. They asked me to read *I Am Human: A Book of Empathy* by Susan Verde and Peter Reynolds, and the publisher donated copies to give away to attendees. We read the book together in what I call a Book-in-Hand storytime, with everyone reading along in their own copy, sharing the experience of making meaning of words, pictures, and design. Afterward, I invited the group to participate in a Family Read-In using a group of books I curated with themes of empathy, solidarity, and pride in Jewish identity. (See the list at the back of this book.)

My ongoing consulting work with groups like EmbraceRace, MERGE for Equality, OurShelves, and Story Starters likewise attempts to support parents and other caregivers in using picture books to facilitate conversations about race, gender, and social justice. Can storytime change the world? I think it can—by asserting messages of equity, inclusion, empathy, and pride, all while creating shared spaces in which to have brave conversations that envision a safer, more humane world for all.

At the end of *Last Stop on Market Street*, Nana tells CJ, "Sometimes when you're surrounded by dirt, CJ, you're a better witness for what's beautiful." Observing children at storytime, promoting discussion, and listening to their voices is the best means I've found in my own life to become "a better witness for what's beautiful." That's why reading *with* children, as opposed to reading *to* them, is such an important part of my practice—at home with my children and in other contexts, too.

PART FOUR

TREASURING WHEN "NOTHING HAPPENS"

I wrote this piece for the Horn Book's Family Reading *blog in 2021 as a post for Pride Month. In it, I embrace the potential for books to help me instill inclusive values in my children so we can bond through a shared worldview that recognizes the humanity of all people.*

I admit I was immediately skeptical when I received a copy of the picture book *Peanut Goes for the Gold* by Jonathan Van Ness of *Queer Eye* fame and Gillian Reid. Though I've watched and enjoyed the show with my teenaged daughters, I have a healthy suspicion of celebrity-penned children's books. My leeriness was coupled with an outright weariness of anthropomorphic animals and objects coded as queer, since publishing seems to prefer such characters over representations of actual queer *people*. So when my youngest children, Jesse (then five) and Zachary (then three), found *Peanut* in a stack of books in my office and asked me to read it with them, they were decidedly more enthusiastic than I was. Nevertheless, I dutifully turned to my tried-and-true Whole Book Approach questions to begin our shared reading.

"Why do you think the endpapers are this color?" I asked, flipping between the yellow endpapers and the jacket art.

"Because it's gold and the letters on the front are gold, too," said Zachary.

"Is Peanut a pirate?" asked Jesse.

"What do you see that makes you say that?" I responded.

"It's not what I see," he explained. "It's those words 'goes for the gold.' Pirates love gold, you know."

"Yeah," said Zachary. "Gold treasure."

"Oh!" I said. "Well, let's find out if Peanut is a pirate." We turned to the first page, and I read the first line of text: "Peanut has their own way of doing things."

"You mean *his* own way," Jesse immediately corrected me.

"No, the words say, '*their* own way,'" I told him. "What do you see that makes you say *his*?"

"I thought the blue shirt," he replied, revealing how he has been socialized to read blue as a visual code for masculine. Then he added, "But look at the shoes!"

"Those are for shes," said Zachary, and Jesse nodded.

In the illustration, Peanut sports a pair of red, high-heeled shoes. They aren't as high as the heels Van Ness often wears on *Queer Eye*, but they are definitely pumps, not flats.

"What do you see about those shoes that makes you think I should say *she* or *her* when I read about Peanut?" I asked.

"Those shoes are clicky like you sometimes wear, and you're a she," said Jesse.

"Right," I said. "But isn't it okay if someone who isn't a she wears clicky shoes?"

"I guess so," said Jesse, while Zachary looked on dubiously.

"Well, I think it's okay," I told them. "And the book says, 'Peanut has *their* own way of doing things,' which means Peanut isn't a boy or a girl. A word for that is *nonbinary*," I explained. "So, instead of saying *he* or *she* or *his* or *hers* when we read about Peanut, we say *they* and *theirs*."

"Oh!" said Jesse. "That's so good for them!"

"Yes!" I said. "That *is* so good for them. And in real life, the only way to know if someone uses *he* or *she* or *them* or some other way to talk about themselves is to learn from them about what is right and to believe them when they tell you."

"I believe Peanut," said Jesse. "I believe them."

As we continued reading, I appreciated how the text is so matter-of-fact in its use of the singular *they*. Not only does this approach normalize the pronoun usage, it holds space for readers to discuss the values that uphold self-determination and resist false gender binaries. I could see Jesse and Zachary working hard to make sure they used the correct pronouns as we talked about Peanut, incorporating this aspect of human diversity into their emerging worldviews.

A few months later, I received the book *The Little Library* by Margaret McNamara and G. Brian Karas. As a longtime Little Free

Library steward at my home, I was excited to share it with my kids. That excitement was reinforced when I realized that this book, too, features a nonbinary character who uses *they/them* pronouns. This time the character is a human—a school librarian named Beck. As in Van Ness's picture book, the text is matter-of-fact in its use of *they*, and this time Jesse and Zachary were unfazed by hearing it read aloud.

"Oh!" I said, once I read a line using *they* to refer to Beck. "The librarian is nonbinary, just like Peanut."

"Yeah, we know," said Jesse. (Translation: "Big whoop.")

"Keep reading," said Zachary.

So I did.

This moment with my kids made me recall author Alex Gino's Stonewall Book Award speech for their middle-grade novel about a transgender girl named Melissa. They delivered it at the 2016 American Library Association annual conference in Orlando, Florida, shortly after the Pulse nightclub shooting, which left forty-nine people dead and fifty-three wounded, most of them queer and Latinx. Gino's speech, available on their website, included the following:

> I have this image that runs through my mind. It takes place 10, 20, 30 years from now. A cisgender, heterosexual, heteronormative, dudey-dude-bro, football playing, fraternity faithful guy is walking down the street. I mean, Dude-Bro. Total stereotype. Drunk as drunk on PBR at 4 in the morning. And in the other direction, walking

towards him, is someone he identifies as trans. And somewhere in his notions and connections of transness, is Melissa's story. And he thinks of Melissa as a person, and he sees the person across the street, and that real, live, possibly-trans person makes it through the night. And nothing happens. Nothing happens.

It's too early to know if either Jesse or Zachary will grow up to be "a cisgender, heterosexual, . . . dudey-dude-bro . . . guy." At this point they seem comfortable with the masculine pronouns assigned them at birth. Thanks in part to books like those about Peanut and Librarian Beck, they also seem comfortable with the fact that not everyone fits into a tidy cisgender binary, which bodes well for their future real-life relationships and interactions with trans and non-binary people.

No, Peanut wasn't a pirate, but the conversation and growth that their story prompted is one I'll always treasure for the "big whoop"/"nothing happens" attitude it inspired when my young sons met Librarian Beck—and I can hardly wait for them to meet Melissa, too.

LOVING BOOK CONVERSATIONS

This piece originally appeared on the EmbraceRace website in 2021. I've become increasingly appreciative of children's books I once might've dismissively called "didactic." Yes, there's a tremendous need for what some call "everyday diversity" or "casual diversity" in children's books, but we also need books for young readers that overtly grapple with racism and other oppressions in historical and contemporary contexts. Such books can bolster confidence, resilience, and empathy in readers, but oftentimes in order for those positive outcomes to be realized, we adults must recognize books as conversation starters, not an end unto themselves.

When I read *Sometimes People March* by Tessa Allen with my then five-year-old son, Jesse, my younger son, Zachary, then almost three, was playing nearby. One thing I most appreciate about this book's sweeping overview of social-justice movements, protests, and the oppressive forces they resist is how it visually connects historical and contemporary events with illustrations of protesters across generations. As we read, I found myself pointing to pictures to explain context to Jesse, saying, for example, "On this page there are people protesting at the Standing Rock Sioux Reservation to resist the Dakota Access Pipeline because building it to bring oil to other parts of the US would poison the water on the land of Indigenous people. That protest happened when you were about one year old."

Then we looked on the facing page. "And over here there's a picture of Mildred and Richard Loving. They lived when it was illegal for a white person and a Black person to get married in their state, and that was a really unfair, racist law or rule. They went to court to change the law, and they won. That happened when your grandmother was still growing up."

Jesse earnestly soaked up what I was sharing with him, and I was grateful for the book's back matter, which helped me answer his questions with specific dates and details. "We march sometimes, too," he said as we closed the book.

"Yes," I said. "When do you remember marching?"

"We went two times to say that families should be together," he said, recalling when our family participated in protests against the Trump administration's policy of family separation at the US–Mexico border. "And we went to Black Lives Matter marches, too," he said.

"Yes, we did. Why do you think we went to those protests and marches?" I asked.

"It's obvious," he said. "Black lives *do* matter. And families *should* be together."

"Right. So we can't just sit around and do nothing if those things aren't obvious to everyone," I said. "And like the book says, 'People are more powerful together.' And 'Sometimes from feelings of fear or anger or injustice comes hope for change.'"

We ended that conversation feeling affirmed and bonded in our shared values and enlightened by Allen's elegantly simple introduction to the need for collective action to effect positive social change.

The next day, Zachary went to my sister's house for the day while Jesse came to my office with me to attend his remote kindergarten class, then in session because of the COVID-19 pandemic. We drove to pick up Zachary afterward, and my sister pulled me aside.

"What's up?" I asked, noting the concern on her face.

"Well, Zachary and I had quite a conversation today," she began.

"About what?" I asked.

"Just out of the blue he said, 'You and Uncle Lee can't be married, Auntie Keita.' I asked him why he would say that, and he said, 'Because you're white and Uncle Lee is Black.'"

"Oh my god," I said, immediately connecting the dots to the conversation Zachary overheard me and Jesse having about the Lovings in *Sometimes People March*. "I'm so sorry."

"I was just really shocked. I mean, I know you obviously aren't teaching him that. I told him that we definitely *can* be married.

He said you read a book that said we couldn't, so I told him that was how it was a long time ago, but that we can be married now because love is love."

"Yes," I said. "Jesse and I were reading a book about protests, and it includes a part about the Loving case and about equal marriage rights for same-sex couples, too," I explained. "He must've been listening more than I thought, but clearly he missed the part about laws changing and historical context."

"Clearly!" said my sister.

After apologizing again, we drove home, and I thought about how to address the matter with Zachary. At the very least, I could pull out our photo album with Keita and Lee's wedding photos, and maybe I'd pull out another picture book, too. I knew we had Selina Alko and Sean Qualls's *The Case for Loving* on our shelves . . . but would that go right over Zachary's not-yet-three-year-old head, too? In the end, Zachary beat me to the punch. That evening, Zachary and I were at the table with Jesse; my husband, Sean; and our then fifteen-year-old, Stevie. Soon after we'd tucked into our meal, Zachary said, "Stevie can't be with us in our family because he is Black, and we are white."

"What?" said Sean.

"I wonder where he got that from," said Stevie.

I jumped in. "No. You're wrong about that, Zachary," I said, and then I turned to Stevie. "I'm really sorry you heard Zachary say that," I told him. "Zachary overheard Jesse and me talking about a book that said that Black and white people couldn't get married a long time ago because of unfair, racist laws, and he's having a hard time understanding what that means for our family now."

I then shared what my sister had told me about her conversation with Zachary earlier that day.

"Wait, he actually said that to her?" asked Stevie incredulously.

"Yes, and she told him that the unfair law changed a long time ago, so now she and Uncle Lee can be married."

"Yeah, and Stevie is our brother, and Rory, Natayja, and Caroline are our siblings, too," said Jesse, referring to their other Black brother and sisters.

"Right," said Sean. "We can all be a family because those laws changed, but there's still a lot that's unfair in our world, so we have to do what we can to help."

"Like march!" said Jesse.

Zachary was quiet for most of this conversation. He didn't seem defensive, or sad, or upset, and there'd been no malice in his statement. He was clearly a confused, very little boy trying to make sense of his world. As much as his preschool-aged mind was grappling with race, he was too young to have reached a point of white fragility that would close him off.

"So do you understand now, Zachary?" I asked. "Like Auntie Keita told you, love is love. And so Stevie and all the kids are just as much a part of this family as you are, and Auntie Keita and Uncle Lee are married, right?"

"Right," said Zachary.

"And I think you should apologize to Stevie in case what you said hurt his feelings," I said.

"I'm sorry, Stevie," said Zachary.

"It's okay," said Stevie.

I knew that this would be just one of many conversations Zachary and I would have about race and racism, working for change, and grappling with history. But honestly I was more concerned about Stevie. As we cleaned up after dinner, I stopped and hugged him and asked, "Are you okay? Even if you understand that Zachary didn't mean to hurt you by saying what he did, I am sorry you had to hear it."

"Yeah, yeah, I'm fine," said Stevie.

I decided to take Stevie at his word and give him space. A few days later, I went up to his room to show him Allen's book. "I've been thinking about our conversation at dinner the other night, and I wanted to know if you have been, too," I began.

"Not really," he said. "But it was really messed up that he said that to Auntie Keita. And it was really messed up he said I couldn't be in this family. I mean, what kind of book were you reading to them?"

"You're right, it is messed up," I said, since clearly he *had* been thinking about the conversation. Now was not the time to defend Zachary or brush aside his remarks. "It was this book that shows people protesting against all kinds of unjust laws and oppression," I explained.

I flipped to the page with the Lovings and showed it to Stevie. "That's the couple whose case challenging the laws against interracial marriage went to the Supreme Court in the 1960s," I told him.

"So why did he think it's still like that?" asked Stevie.

I decided to give him my perspective, since he'd asked. "I think because he's not yet three, so he doesn't really understand how time works and what it means that a law was in force 'a long time ago.' Also, I think he got stuck on the shock of a rule that could go against our family in so many ways."

We talked for a while longer, and I asked if there was anything he wished I'd done differently to handle our dinnertime conversation, or to follow up with him, or with Zachary.

"I guess the only thing I wish you did differently was maybe not to read that book to Zachary in the first place. He obviously didn't get it."

"Fair," I said. "Or maybe what I should've done was involve him more in the reading and conversation. Part of the reason he didn't get it was because he didn't talk with Jesse and me about the book. He just heard parts and misinterpreted it."

"Yeah, and he got the total opposite of what the book was trying to say," said Stevie.

He had a point!

This conversation with Stevie left me feeling grateful to him for trusting me enough to share his thoughts and feelings. It also reinforced my awareness of the importance of discussing books I read with my kids, perhaps particularly those that are overtly didactic, instead of just reading them and leaving it at that.

On the fifty-fourth anniversary of the Loving case, I reread *Sometimes People March* with Zachary, who was three and a half by then. We stopped at the page with the illustration of the Lovings, and I told him, "A long time ago, before Mommy was born, it was against the law for a Black person and a white person to be married in the state where these people named Mildred and Richard Loving lived. That was not fair, and so they helped change that law so now couples like Auntie Keita and Uncle Lee can be married anywhere in our country. Isn't that good?"

"Yes!" said Zachary.

"So Black people and white people can marry each other if they want to now, right?" I asked, to make absolutely certain he got it this time.

"Yes!"

"And that is good because love is . . ." I paused to let him fill in the blank, wondering if he'd remember the line "love is love" that his auntie had used or if he'd fill in another positive word. Instead, he said,

". . . gross!"

I laughed out loud. "No, Zachary," I said. "Love is the best thing in the world."

"Well, Jesse and I think love is gross," he said.

"No way," I said. "Love is love is love is love! And that's why it's so good that we don't have those unfair laws anymore."

"Unfair is not loving," said Zachary.

"Right. So what if you notice something unfair? What can you say or do about it?"

"Stop it!" said Zachary.

"And what if you do something unfair and someone tells you to stop it?"

"I can say sorry," said Zachary.

"Is it gross for me to say I love you?" I asked.

"No," said Zachary. "Love is love."

Marching isn't the only way to create change, of course. Sometimes people offer trust. Sometimes people apologize. Sometimes people forgive. Sometimes people have hard conversations. Sometimes people speak. Sometimes people listen. Sometimes people grow. Sometimes people read and discuss books. I'm grateful for books like Allen's that can foster conversations to support all of these means toward change on personal and broader levels, if only we stop to have them.

CROSSING BRIDGES, TURNING PAGES

Since this piece documents less-than-rosy parts of parenting, I shared it with the child it's focused on before sending it to the Horn Book's Family Reading *blog in 2018 in order to make sure I didn't overstep any boundaries. I noted that I used the singular* they *throughout the piece in order to avoid identifying them and said that I didn't write this to shame or expose them in any way. "Fine," they said. "And we never even finished listening to that book, you know," they said, referencing Markus Zusak's* The Book Thief, *which I discuss in the essay. That's true! But whether we finish every book we start together or not, connecting with each other through books is one way of easing relationship ups and downs.*

Mothering my seven children often inspires my writing, but I've made it a policy to avoid writing publicly about specific struggles I have with my kids. Growing up is hard enough, and I worry that too much openness could amount to betrayal or worse. All this to say: I have a story about one of my kids and how reading together helped us find our way back to each other.

It was a rough year, and I felt that this child, with whom I had shared a deep closeness in the past, was slipping away from me. Communication with their school told me things weren't much better there.

Hurt people hurt people. I know this. And though I don't know all the reasons for it, I know my child's deep hurts caused them to lash out. It made me want to lash back, especially when my other kids were in the line of fire, and a few awful times I did. I have excellent co-parenting support that made me feel less alone as I tried to make things better. We sought outside help, but nothing broke through. Negative consequences (grounding, loss of privileges, etc.) increased anger, sadness, and isolation, which in turn exacerbated power struggles. It was a vicious, exhausting cycle.

I sometimes mustered the energy and clarity of mind to flip the script, and instead of sending them to their room for a time-out (frankly, as respite for myself), I instituted what I call "time-ins." I started doing this with real intention when I realized that although I read every day with my two youngest children, it'd been a long time since I'd done so with any of my five older kids.

I hope books will show my child a path through all the inner turmoil. But I don't expressly give them books about kids struggling with issues similar to theirs, nor do I seek out stories in which parents and kids butt heads and come through to the other side. No, I simply share books that I hope they will love as a means of expressing my love for them, and I offer books up like hugs, Band-Aids, comfort food, apologies, and bridges.

I used a work trip as an opportunity for a daylong time-in. I said they could read on their own while I took care of work obligations, but I asked them to choose an audiobook for us to listen to in the car during the four-hour round trip.

"Let's do *The Book Thief*," they said. "You put it on my shelf, but I never read it because I thought it looked cheesy."

"Why?" I asked.

"I thought the title meant it was about someone who loves books so much that they steal them. And that seemed . . . cheesy. Like, I get it: books are great."

Fair enough.

We got about a quarter of the way through the audiobook during our drive, pausing to talk about various points of World War II–era history that they didn't grasp, marveling over the skill of audiobook reader Allan Corduner, and grappling with the text's references to African American Olympic gold medalist Jesse Owens and how author Markus Zusak handles race.

Reflecting back on that day lets me see how listening to this book together provided a buffer between us that paradoxically allowed us to connect. I saw my child's mind at work and delighted in the insights and questions that bubbled forth, seeing evidence of the intelligence and depth that are and will be their best tools for getting through hard times. We didn't talk about anything in our own lives, nor about their struggles at school. It was such a relief. We didn't ever turn back to *The Book Thief* together, though I encouraged my child to finish the book on their own.

We did read *The Girl Who Drank the Moon* by Kelly Barnhill, which I read aloud to them and a sibling. The sibling was delighted to have this renewed shared reading time, but despite the book's brilliance, I wouldn't call my other child's participation enthusiastic. While I read, I had to ignore many exasperated sighs about the forced time-in and a lot of hiding in a hoodie and pretending not to listen. This was not the idyllic scene of mother-and-child shared reading that I had lived out with this child in the past, nor that their sibling enacts, rapt beside me with repeated entreaties to read just one more chapter. But (and yes, I look really, really hard for signs of connection) I also noticed their posture relax as I read aloud. It felt a little like that day in the car listening to *The Book Thief.* It felt like what Mem Fox calls "reading magic." It was still there. It was still working.

Given the busyness of our lives, it was a slow process to read *The Girl Who Drank the Moon* together. I itched to read ahead so I could finish the story for myself. I waited for them, however, because I wanted this book to hold its magical tale of Luna; and Xan, Glerk, and Fyrian; *and* the story of us finding respite in its pages, too.

I've been a mother for over half my life. My eldest child is now past the age I was when he was born. My youngest won't reach that age for a long time. The not-so-funny thing about parenting so many children is that, at least for me, it doesn't get easier with practice. They're all so different from one another. They have their own needs, strengths, challenges, histories, and dynamics with me and other family members. But so far, decades into this mothering life of mine, I've found that books offer a consistent means of connecting with my kids, even when (or perhaps especially when) other means fail us.

The child at the center of this essay would probably say all this is cheesy—"Like, I get it: books are great"—but that's okay. I'm not trying to convince them of anything, except that we can always turn the page.

THE BOOK OF MISTAKES
SETS US FREE

This essay began as a Calling Caldecott *blog at the* Horn Book *in 2017 focused on Corinna Luyken's stunning debut,* The Book of Mistakes. *Here I've expanded my reflection to include commentary about how very special this book is because of how it speaks to one of my daughters and to me, bridging the gaps between us.*

My daughter Caroline is a sensitive person who deeply—it often seems daily—feels a full range of emotions. She's also a gifted artist, and she has a strong perfectionist streak. This is a tough combination. I remember watching an old episode of *Sesame Street* with her when she was about four that included a clip of the Muppet pianist, Don Music, crashing his head against the keys in despair over a missed note. *Oh my god*, I thought, with a jolt of recognition. *That's my kid.*

Caroline never actually bashed her head against the table over a mistake, but she'd crumple up papers, burst into tears, and make what Ramona Quimby fans might describe as a "great big noisy fuss" when frustration mounted. After witnessing one such outburst, my mother said, "It's like every day she wakes up, straps on a pair of roller skates, and starts heading uphill."

I wouldn't have her any other way.

Our world needs people who hold themselves to high standards, who feel deeply, and who channel their emotions and ideas into artistic expressions that allow other—perhaps less sensitive—people to see things new ways. The flip side of Caroline's self-destructive perfectionist tendencies is that artmaking has always been a therapeutic outlet for her, a means of expressing herself and venting her big emotions. I ache for my girl when she's hard on herself, even as I value how she wears her tender heart on her sleeve. I've tried to find ways to keep her from getting hurt by what Langston Hughes called "the too-rough fingers / Of the world" in his poem "The Dream Keeper." Especially when those fingers are on her very own hand.

How I wish we'd had Corinna Luyken's debut picture book, *The Book of Mistakes*, years ago. It's a masterful celebration of the creative process, and its central premise—that so-called mistakes are opportunities for creative inspiration—can serve as a powerful antidote to the sort of inhibiting and overwhelming perfectionism that punctuates my daughter's life.

Beyond its worthy messages for kids like my daughter, *The Book of Mistakes* is a picture book I immediately adored for its artistic merits. Storytimes have deepened my admiration of Luyken's achievement. When I read this book with a sixth-grade class, they had a lot to say about the layout, jacket, and cover.

First they noted how the jacket includes a small depiction of a Black boy looking up at children floating away with balloons.

"He got left behind," one child said.

"So that's the mistake of the story," concluded another.

"And maybe now he's going to try to get to them?" speculated a classmate.

"Or they'll come back for him," added someone else.

Another child turned attention to the display type and the plural noun, *mistakes*. They said, "Another mistake is that the balloons broke the title."

When we took the jacket off to examine the cover underneath, there was palpable delight in the room. The students noted that the left-behind boy's unicycle is outfitted with its own big balloon.

"That's how he'll get to them!" exclaimed one child, and the stage was set for them to test their theories about the narrative. But before getting to the opening spread, we paused at the endpapers, an empty expanse of white with two inkblots marring them.

"Those are more mistakes," said one student.

"And they're in the same places as the balloon kids and the unicycle boy," observed another. And so they are. This minimal design introduces the inkblot motif that appears on other pages. The inkblots reach for upper and lower heights to emphasize space, movement, and perspective—elements that are key to following and interpreting this visual story.

The first image inside the book is an incomplete sketch of a face with one eye, one ear, a nose, and a tiny suggestion of an eyebrow. "It started," reads the accompanying text, and a page turn completes the sentence, "with one mistake." Now the face has a line for a mouth; some penciled-in hair; another tiny eyebrow; and a too-big, black circle of an eye, far larger than the small one on the prior page. Readers can now name the mistake themselves. It's an easy task that prepares readers for closer examination of the increasingly complex spreads that follow.

As one "mistake" after another gives way to new artistic inspiration, Luyken presents artmaking as a series of problems to solve. It's not a slog but a process that demands a playful mindset fed by missteps. Meanwhile, the pages with "mistakes," like one with "[t]he elbow and the extra-long neck" provoke laughter at storytime. Kids understand Luyken's fast-and-loose play with proportions. Clearly she's an artist who can break the rules for humorous effect.

The drawing eventually becomes a girl wearing roller skates, and the sixth graders I read with recognized her as one of the children sailing away on the front of the jacket. This connection returned them to their initial theories about the boy who'd been left behind and whether he'd try to catch up with them. It also made them wonder about the balloons and where all the other kids were. Luyken soon delivers those details. The result is wish fulfillment of the readerly sort—we get what we expect, but we get much more, too. The balloons? They're delivered by the roller-skating girl on wordless spreads that invite the reader to narrate her quirky progress toward a massive tree. The other children? They're swarming, climbing, and cavorting among the tree's branches.

I can't quite capture the rich responses of kids at storytime to the other shifts in *The Book of Mistakes*, but I heard a lot of gasps and "wows" and "whoas" and other exclamations of sheer delight. Especially when the shadowy landscape ends up being the helmeted head of the roller-skating girl, and perspective zooms back out to cast her as an artist who's drawing the same slight sketches that started the book.

"It's her! She's the artist!"

"She's drawing herself!"

The sixth graders I read with weren't disappointed that the unicycle boy ended up sailing off with the kids, as they had predicted. They were delighted by the turn of events that led them to speculate that the girl in the book is Luyken herself.

"Since the girl in the book is the one making the pictures of herself and everything, it's like she's the real artist. We're seeing how the real artist thinks," one child said.

This seems an ideal encapsulation of what this picture book does so exceptionally well: it *captures* Luyken's imaginative, creative process in order to *set free* the imaginations of her readers.

And when I think of my daughter Caroline's response to this book, I can't help but connect my mother's comment about her roller-skating uphill with the image of the roller-skating girl. On the surface, they both have a wicked-cool fashion sense. The book character's high lace collar, striped leggings, pink skates, black helmet, and aqua goggles would fit right in with Caroline's eclectic wardrobe. Starting on the first day of kindergarten, neighborhood parents giddily anticipated what my daughter would show up wearing at the bus stop each morning. She uses her body like a canvas, expressing her individuality and rejecting distinctions between Halloween costumes and school clothes, between accessories and necessities.

In sixth grade, Caroline decided to get braid extensions for the first time, after seeing her older sisters with them. She chose a bright reddish color, kept the sides of her head shaved, and said she loved the results because it looked "cool and crazy and wild." I thought she looked amazing, and so like *herself*. But sadly, for the first time that I recall, she crumbled under social pressure when some kids teased her about the sudden change. She took out the braids, and I worried about how social pressures would continue to impact her sense of self.

It's a small thing, but I'm glad she's vowed to never outgrow picture books. She finds comfort in them and inspiration, too. Time and again I've found her poring over Luyken's book. It clearly occupies a special place in her big, artistic heart.

"What's your takeaway from this book, Caroline?" I asked her.

"I like how it uses mistakes to make art. And how it says that if you mess up, it's not really a problem," she responded.

"Is that how you feel when you make art?" I wondered.

"Not really," she admitted with chagrin. "But I like the idea."

I can't remember what provoked the outburst that made Caroline stomp off to her room one day, yelling, "I hate everybody!"

When she came back downstairs, she said, "I was mad, so I ripped this box, and then I realized it was the perfect thing to make a scenery. So I made a desert."

She showed me a diorama of sorts, with a torn-paper collage of bright-yellow sand and sky, two green cacti, and a scorpion with a tail she'd curled with a pair of scissors. I could see how the act of tearing paper was in and of itself satisfying. In her work I saw the heat of the desert as symbolic of her anger, the cacti and scorpion representing her prickly, get-away-from-me rage, and the whole thing as an exercise in apology and reconciliation—an effort to make something good out of the bad. Throwing a fit isn't quite the same as making a mistake, but the therapeutic process of channeling bad feelings into creativity seems similar somehow. I think this is another reason that Luyken's meditation on art-making resonates so powerfully with Caroline.

"Set your imagination free"—the fine type on the back of *The Book of Mistakes*' jacket—begs the question, "Free from what?" In Caroline's case, I think the struggle is to free her imagination from her perfectionism and from others' judgment so she can express herself as an artist and envision and embody her own true self. My parenting ideal is to guide and support her and all her siblings in this struggle. I don't wish to mold my children into my vision for them, nor to aim them like arrows at specific targets. Instead, I want to see them as the individuals they are, help them follow the paths they choose, and see them become the adults they are meant to be. It's not revelatory to admit that this is hard work. To borrow my mother's analogy, it can be like roller-skating uphill.

It sometimes feels like I'm failing at my ideal and making mistake after mistake after mistake—

Wait.

This sounds familiar.

I didn't know I'd end up writing about myself when I began this piece about my daughter and how important *The Book of Mistakes* is to her, but here I am, doing just that. Another reason I love this book is that it resonates with me as an adult engaged in the messy art of parenting. Caroline's perfectionist streak may keep her metaphorically roller-skating uphill in much of her (creative) life. Seeing Luyken's freer, gentler approach to creativity embodied by a roller-skating, drawing girl provides Caroline with a model for being a little less hard on herself. It helps her level that hill she climbs each day, embracing her own artist self—no matter how others might respond.

THE BOY RAMONA

I wrote this essay way back in 2010 for the Horn Book's *Family Reading blog. Starting with my eldest son, Rory, my children's reading lives have often defied gender stereotypes. For example, my sons are avid readers and my daughters are not. The girls always liked shared reading with me, and they do read independently, but they aren't the voracious and varied readers that their brothers are. In Rory's case, there was a time I worried that reading was becoming too much of a good thing. But . . . I got over that.*

After a particularly hard day at school, my then nine-year-old son Rory forlornly and aptly announced, "I think I'm the *boy* Ramona."

Rory turned to books and characters for escape and solace as he set out to slay the particular dragon that he shared with Beverly Cleary's protagonist: school. Despite being a very bright kid with all sorts of strengths and talents, Rory felt unsuccessful in school.

Like Ramona Quimby, Rory often seemed to be a proverbial square peg trying to fit into a round hole.

Unlike Ramona, he's a boy, biracial, has anything but a traditional family, and reading, not drawing, is his passion. Rory quite suddenly became an early expert reader at the end of kindergarten. One day he couldn't read, and the next it was like a light switch went on, and he could read just about anything. This served him well as a first grader, where he struggled as mightily as Ramona the Brave to feel liked by his teacher and to meet her expectations.

"I just want to play! To read and to play," he sobbed one night when he came home with a fat packet of math worksheets.

"Of course you do," I told him. "You're six."

But something else was bothering Rory that day. The same precocious reading ability that enabled him to feel better about himself had also made him privy to a four-letter word scrawled in a bathroom stall.

"Mom-Mom," he said to me, using the name he'd given to me as a baby, "I read that word, and I am just so worried I'm going to *say* it!"

"Well," I said. I took a cue from the Quimbys, who famously gave a frustrated, angry Ramona permission to say a "bad word" as she vented about a rotten day in first grade. "What would happen if you did say it, Rory?"

He was shocked. "You'd be mad?" he posited.

"Well, I wouldn't want you to run around saying it to be rude or mean, but whatever it is, I think you should say the bad word now, so it doesn't seem so scary."

Rory did not say *guts* (Ramona's bad word). Rory said *fuck*. He said it two more times, then burst into tears of relief.

"You see?" I told him. "It's just a word."

The next day, I told Rory's teacher about the graffiti, and she connected the dots and told me that Rory had been avoiding the bathroom. I ached for him, scared to death by a word on a wall on top of all his other anxieties, and I rethought the reassurance that I'd given him the day before: "It's just a word."

Words were, and are, everything to Rory. He delights in learning them, saying them, writing them, and hearing them, but mostly he revels in reading them, and it's been one of my greatest pleasures to foster his reading life. For a time, though, I worried about the overpowering nature of books in his life.

Rory's very first word was—no kidding—*book*. At about ten months old, he began insistently blurting out "buh, buh, buh" while climbing up on my lap. I like to think I set the stage for this auspicious piece of vocabulary acquisition when Rory was a newborn. My mother joked that he was the youngest member of Oprah's Book Club when I, an earnest first-time mother determined to do everything right, told her that I read aloud to him from novels while he was breastfeeding so that he'd be "exposed to rich language."

Our shared reading, of course, also included plenty of board books and picture books in those baby days, and we started adding chapter books to the mix when he was in preschool. We kept reading together even after he was able to read by himself, not only for the comfortable ritual of bedtime reading but also for the closeness the time afforded us, especially as our family expanded to include one, then two, then four younger siblings by the time Rory was nine.

By then, however, Rory had begun to assert more independence than I was ready to accept. "Don't you want to read with us?" I'd ask him while curling up with a stack of picture books or a read-aloud favorite like *The House at Pooh Corner* or *The Animal Family* to share with his younger brother and sisters at bedtime.

"I'd rather just read by myself" or "I've already read that with you" became his standard replies.

After all, he could read and reread much more quickly on his own, and his preferences were straying far from the sorts of books his siblings and I were apt to choose. Comics, graphic novels, and plot-driven fantasies were his literary cups of tea, and he drained the dregs and looked for more.

Notice I didn't say *asked* for more. For years, and much to my chagrin, Rory rejected my eager book recommendations at the library, in bookstores, and at home.

"Read this," I said, thrusting Louis Sachar's *Holes* at him one day when he was ten. "You'll love it."

"It doesn't look so good to me," he replied. "I'm rereading the Warriors series now."

"Rory, I do know what I'm talking about, you know. It's sort of my job to know about good kids' books," I said, trying to assert the authority of my children's-literature-professor status.

I should have known better.

"Mom-Mom, you haven't even finished Harry Potter five, and I've already read book seven. Twice."

He had me there. I hadn't (and still haven't) finished the Harry Potter series. Nor have I read all (or in some cases, any) of the books in the other fantasy series that gripped Rory's attention: Rick Riordan's Percy Jackson series, Suzanne Collins's Underland Chronicles, Brian Jacques's Redwall books, D. J. MacHale's Pendragon series, and yes, Erin Hunter's Warriors. Battling clans of talking cats? Really? Really.

Rory has read and reread these books, and many others (including, I am happy to say, *Holes*), countless times. He can recite passages from favorite books, and he recounts favorite lines at will—sometimes when a totally separate conversation is going on around him. This started to become troubling, especially when the Harry Potter audiobooks seemed to take up a bit too much brain space—space where remembering to bring home books for assignments, or focusing on math, or even just finding his shoes in the morning might have come in handy.

"It's like he's so focused on the stories in his head that he can't shift gears to get on top of everything else," I said to a neuropsychologist when Rory was in third grade. We consulted him about Rory's ongoing struggle to make sense of school despite IQ tests that revealed "overpowering intellectual abilities."

"Most schools aren't made for kids like Rory," the doctor told me. "His brain is like a huge library, filled with passions, images, words, and ideas, but the library is completely disorganized, and he can't readily access its resources because the catalog is down, and the librarian is on a lunch break."

We set to work on a plan to get Rory's metaphorical library back in order and to check in with that out-to-lunch librarian residing in his brain. I told the doctor, "I want Rory to be Rory, and I want him to feel okay about the things that make him different." Rory developed a passion for reading the *New Yorker* at eight (mostly for the cartoons, true), and by the same age, he thought that NPR's *A Prairie Home Companion* and *Car Talk* (along with Calvin and Hobbes and Dav Pilkey's *The Adventures of Captain Underpants*) were the height of humor.

I wanted to help Rory function, and I also didn't want him to lose his ability to become so consumed by reading that the rest of the world became, to borrow the word he used to describe math class, irrelevant. Testing eventually resulted in a diagnosis of ADHD, inattentive type. The disorder did not manifest itself in Rory with hyperactivity but with a checked-out, spacey way of being in the world much of the time. Often incidents were related to his passion for reading. For example, during a parent-teacher conference in third grade, his teacher voiced concern about Rory's penchant for "disappearing" from the classroom at random times during the day.

"He'll just get up and leave without asking," he explained.

Where did Rory go? To the library, of course.

"How is it that he can focus so deeply on books and retain their words and meanings, but he can't focus on things like directions and interactions in the real world?" I asked the neuropsychologist.

"Well, as hard as it is for him right now to navigate the outer world, think about what a rich inner world he has."

Those words were balm to my weary, worried mother's soul. I hadn't thought of his reading life as an inner sanctuary from the confounding outer world that he faced every day, where most kids were round pegs nestled snugly in round holes.

I recalled the doctor's words often as I watched Rory become a young man. With help from his teachers, doctors, and family, but mostly through his ability to turn inward and to reflect on who he is and who he wants to be, Rory made tremendous strides. Like any adolescent, he had bouts of angst, frustration, and self-doubt, but he really came into his own and is a keenly self-aware and insightful adult.

As has always been true, books help Rory gain insights into himself. Inspired by Jeff Kinney's Diary of a Wimpy Kid series, Rory began keeping a journal when he started middle school. He invited me to read the first entry; it had as much to do with the books he was reading as it did with navigating his place in our blended family, in his school, and in the life he imagined for himself in the future. In one part, he reflected on reading Sherman Alexie's *The Absolutely True Diary of a Part-Time Indian*. "That Arnold Spirit—he's a really brave kid," Rory said to me when we talked about what he had written.

I saw many connections between him and Arnold, despite their wildly different biographies and respective sets of challenges in school and in life. My "boy Ramona" saw himself in Cleary's character and it seemed he'd also found himself in Alexie's. Rory was a really brave kid, too, daring every day to be himself. It might've been easier to cave and pretend to be someone who didn't love the History Channel or who didn't have a passion for geography, manga, and languages, prompting him to try to teach himself Japanese and to declare himself an "aspiring Shinto."

I think that he got this strength, in part, because of the rich inner world of reading and rereading that he built for himself; a world that is populated by similarly quirky, bright, and sensitive kids. Kids like Arnold and Ramona, yes, but also like Harry Potter, Joey Pigza, Percy Jackson, George and Harold, and on and on.

And no matter what paths Rory's life takes, I know he will always be a reader.

DRAWING COMFORT
FROM SHARED READING

I wrote this piece for the Horn Book *in 2020 during the COVID-19 pandemic, amid the longest separation I'd ever had from my oldest son. I set out to reflect on the staying power of book bonding even when our children are adults. Educator Peter Carolin read the essay and offered his interpretation of my piece, noting how book bonding is often rooted in repeat readings. He wrote in part, "You imply with your idyllic moment the importance of repeating/creating a refrain, so a reunification may take place of past, present, and future; heart, mind, and soul. Thank you."*

I saw my eldest son, Rory, in person at Boston's Isabella Stewart Gardner Museum in February 2020. He performed in the opening event for the exhibit "Boston's Apollo: Thomas McKeller and John

Singer Sargent." Rory's role was to read McKeller's letters as part of a multifaceted performance of dance and music. As I watched my son hold his own among world-class pianists, singers, and dancers, I had moments of seeing his child-self within his adult face and form and of hearing his boyish voice beneath the rich baritone that seems to come from the soles of his feet, never mind his chest.

He's still in there, I thought, not in a spirit of infantilizing my grown-up son but of marveling at how the child I'd nurtured and fed, read to and cheered on, had grown into a man living out his dreams.

And then COVID-19 pulled the rug out from under Rory, as it did so many others. Though he remained physically healthy, the disruption of the post-college life he loved and worked hard to build took an emotional toll. We stayed in close touch while I hunkered down at home across the state with my husband and four of my other kids, and I sent him care packages with books that he couldn't bring his spinning mind to read. Then, in early June, Rory texted in a state of raw need and vulnerability provoked by the wave of racialized violence coinciding with the pandemic. He'd participated in two protests following George Floyd's murder by Minneapolis police and was overcome by anger, sadness, fear, and despair. At one point he mentioned something that brought him comfort, saying, "I took a nap today and had a dream that you were reading a bedtime story to me."

We quickly switched to FaceTime, and I pulled some of his childhood books from my shelves to read aloud. Mindful of Rory's immediate need to feel safe and nurtured as a young Black man, I began with a poem I'd read to him countless times when he was little because of how it evoked my hopes for him as a Black child: Walter Dean Myers's "Prayer" from *Brown Angels: An Album of Pictures and Verse*. It includes the lines:

For I am dark and precious
And have such gifts to give

"I remember that one!" said Rory. "Read it again."

Read it again.

How many times had Rory said those words to me over the years? And how many years had it been since he'd said them? Many, on both counts. I somehow managed not to cry as I reread "Prayer" and then flipped back to share Myers's full collection before revisiting other picture books with my son. In later weeks he requested more FaceTime storytimes, and I happily, gratefully obliged to offer his hurting heart comfort and affirmation from a hundred miles away.

One night we read Ashley Bryan's *Beautiful Blackbird*. We didn't get much past the personalized inscription Bryan had written to Rory on the title page before I heard my then two-year-old, Zachary, loudly resisting bedtime in the next room. I scooped him up and brought him into my office, saying, "I'm reading a book to Rory on the phone. Do you want to read, too?"

"Sure!" said Zachary, astonished at his good fortune.

Soon, he and Rory were reading along with me, repeating the refrain, "Black is beautiful, UH-HUH!"

Overhearing us, sixteen-year-old Emilia walked in and asked, "What are you doing?"

"Reading with Rory," I said. "Do you want to join us?"

"Okay," said Emilia, pulling Zachary into her lap.

It was a pretty idyllic experience, one I held on to while also holding concerns about how the incredibly difficult time of the pandemic would impact each of my children's "wondrous life to live," as Myers's "Prayer" says.

A wise friend said her primary parenting focus during the pandemic was on what her children's "emotional memory" of the time will be. I tried to take that perspective to heart, knowing I can't fix everything and being woefully aware of the times when stress and worry have gotten the best of me. It's hard not to despair or to feel helpless in the face of so much uncertainty and pain.

But writers and artists like Bryan, Myers, and others have helped me stay connected with my children, even in the most difficult times. For that, I'm grateful, not just because of the immediate comfort that shared reading can provide but because of the lasting impressions it makes. It's part of the child that's "still in there" when I see my grown son onstage or on FaceTime and with me in person again.

AFTERWORD

I was a Black kid who grew up in a predominantly white town. It was inevitable I would run into contradictions between my identity and the place in which I lived. I felt isolated from a community of Black people with whom I could bond over common experiences, and becoming truly conscious of my race was kind of like finding out Santa isn't real, but with higher stakes. Suddenly I realized that society applies caveats to my humanity, my appearance is seen as abnormal, and I will always need to disprove others' presumptions about me.

Thankfully my mother made certain to fill my life with enriching stories by Black authors like Virginia Hamilton, Julius Lester, Walter Dean Myers, and Jerry and Brian Pinkney, and featuring Black characters like John Henry. From folktales to poetry and slice-of-life picture books, these books proved extremely important to me. This type of literature is something I could've come across and enjoyed on my own, but what really reinforced its value was the fact that my mom read to me, and she exposed me to these authors and books at an early age. My ADHD-addled brain fixates on narratives like nothing else, and my perspective of myself and the world around me would have been significantly narrower without exposure to the books my mother shared with me.

As I started reading on my own, I was drawn to fantasy and comics. Unfortunately, these genres in particular left me inundated by literature that seemed to always lack Black characters and had very few Black protagonists, so I grew up inserting them into what I read. This was a healthy exercise in overcoming social alienation, a phenomenon experienced by people everywhere, especially as communities and cultures are redefined by economic and climate conditions. When our social experience doesn't reflect who we perceive ourselves to be, we need something to grab on to, and imagination is one of the most powerful tools at our disposal.

Despite my positive efforts to read myself into the books I loved, in retrospect I have another argument with many childhood favorites. I don't mean to sound cynical, but from *The Phantom Tollbooth* to Harry Potter, I think the biggest falsehood in children's literature is that life is inherently meaningful, fulfilling, and guided by unambiguous morals. In real life, the path of "the chosen one" or "the hero's journey" has much more to do with one's race and class position than being naturally special. A society captured by capitalism accounts for human well-being and meaningful social experiences only as far as they benefit short-term profit. (Why yes, I am a Gen-Z college graduate living in a northeastern city—why do you ask?) In this context, I've come to think the best thing anyone can do is recognize that they're not a protagonist in their own hero's journey but a secondary character in countless others' stories.

Bonding with my mother over books prepared me for this outlook by instilling in me an appreciation for the enormous range of lived experiences I have encountered and a natural curiosity about the world around me. While imagination can help us resist the limitations of the world as it is, curiosity makes the world a much larger and more beautiful place by allowing us to see beyond ourselves. I still try to learn something new every day, and if I have children of my own (or the opportunity to mentor children), I hope I can inspire this type of curiosity in them as well, by bonding with them through books.

Rory Lambert-Wright
Boston, MA, 2022

Lists of Books

BOOKS AND SERIES MENTIONED IN THESE ESSAYS
(alphabetical by title)

Absolutely True Diary of a Part-Time Indian, The by Sherman Alexie, illustrated by Ellen Forney

Adrian Simcox Does NOT Have a Horse by Marcy Campbell, illustrated by Corinna Luyken

Adventures of Captain Underpants, The by Dav Pilkey

All American Boys by Jason Reynolds and Brendan Kiely

And If the Moon Could Talk by Kate Banks, illustrated by Georg Hallensleben

Animal Family, The by Randall Jarrell, illustrated by Maurice Sendak

Astronaut Annie by Suzanne Slade, illustrated by Nicole Tadgell

At the Mountain's Base by Traci Sorell (Cherokee), illustrated by Weshoyot Alvitre (Tongva and Scottish)

Auggie & Me: Three Wonder Stories by R. J. Palacio

Beautiful Blackbird by Ashley Bryan

Ben's Trumpet by Rachel Isadora

Birchbark House, The by Louise Erdrich (Turtle Mountain Chippewa)

Birdsong by Julie Flett (Cree-Métis)

Black Is Brown Is Tan by Arnold Adoff, illustrated by Emily Arnold McCully

Bone by Jeff Smith

Book of Mistakes, The by Corinna Luyken

Book Thief, The by Markus Zusak

Boss Baby, The by Marla Frazee

Brave Irene by William Steig

Bridge to Terabithia by Katherine Paterson

Brown Angels: An Album of Pictures and Verse by Walter Dean Myers

Calvin and Hobbes series by Bill Watterson

Case for Loving, The: The Fight for Interracial Marriage by Selina Alko, illustrated by Sean Qualls and Selina Alko

Child Is Born, A by Margaret Wise Brown, illustrated by Floyd Cooper

Child's Christmas in Wales, A by Dylan Thomas, illustrated by Trina Schart Hyman

Chrysanthemum by Kevin Henkes

Counting the Stars: The Story of Katherine Johnson, NASA Mathematician by Lesa Cline-Ransome and Raúl Colón

Cushla and Her Books by Dorothy Butler

Dave the Potter: Artist, Poet, Slave by Laban Carrick Hill, illustrated by Bryan Collier

Dear Martin by Nic Stone

Diary of a Wimpy Kid series by Jeff Kinney

Drawn Together by Minh Lê, illustrated by Dan Santat

Dream Keeper and Other Poems, The by Langston Hughes, illustrated by Brian Pinkney

Eloise by Kay Thompson, illustrated by Hilary Knight

Farmer and the Circus, The by Marla Frazee

Farmer and the Clown, The by Marla Frazee

Farmer and the Monkey, The by Marla Frazee

57 Bus, The: A True Story of Two Teenagers and the Crime That Changed Their Lives by Dashka Slater

First Christmas, The by Tomie dePaola

Flora & Ulysses: The Illuminated Adventures by Kate DiCamillo, illustrated by K. G. Campbell

Flora's Very Windy Day by Jeanne Birdsall, illustrated by Matt Phelan

Gardener, The by Sarah Stewart, illustrated by David Small

George and Martha series by James Marshall

Girl Who Drank the Moon, The by Kelly Barnhill

Glorious Day, A by Amy Schwartz

Go the F*ck to Sleep by Adam Mansbach, illustrated by Ricardo Cortés

Grump by Janet S. Wong, illustrated by John Wallace

Guess How Much I Love You by Sam McBratney, illustrated by Anita Jeram

Harriet, You'll Drive Me Wild! by Mem Fox, illustrated by Marla Frazee

Harry Potter series by J. K. Rowling

Heather Has Two Mommies by Lesléa Newman, illustrated by Laura Cornell

Henry's Freedom Box: A True Story from the Underground Railroad by Ellen Levine, illustrated by Kadir Nelson

Hey Black Child by Useni Eugene Perkins, illustrated by Bryan Collier

Holes by Louis Sachar

Homemade Love by bell hooks, illustrated by Shane W. Evans

Honey, I Love and Other Love Poems by Eloise Greenfield, illustrated by Leo and Diane Dillon

House at Pooh Corner, The by A. A. Milne, illustrated by Ernest H. Shepard

How the Heather Looks: A Joyous Journey to the British Sources of Children's Books by Joan Bodger

How I Became a Ghost: A Choctaw Trail of Tears Story by Tim Tingle (Choctaw)

Hundred Dresses, The by Eleanor Estes, illustrated by Louis Slobodkin

I Am Human: A Book of Empathy by Susan Verde, illustrated by Peter H. Reynolds

I Love You, Stinky Face by Lisa McCourt, illustrated by Cyd Moore

I Want My Hat Back by Jon Klassen

Ida B. Wells-Barnett: Strike a Blow Against a Glaring Evil by Anne Schraff

Indian Shoes by Cynthia Leitich Smith (Muscogee)

Interrupting Chicken by David Ezra Stein

Joey Pigza series by Jack Gantos

John Henry by Julius Lester, illustrated by Jerry Pinkney

King & King by Linda de Haan and Stern Nijland

Knuffle Bunny Too: A Case of Mistaken Identity by Mo Willems

Last Stop on Market Street by Matt de la Peña, illustrated by Christian Robinson

Little House on the Prairie series by Laura Ingalls Wilder, illustrated by Garth Williams

Little Library, The by Margaret McNamara, illustrated by G. Brian Karas

Little You by Richard Van Camp (Dogrib Tłįcho), illustrated by Julie Flett (Cree-Métis)

Prophet, The by Khalil Gibran

Raisin in the Sun, A by Lorraine Hansberry

Ramona the Brave by Beverly Cleary

Reading Magic: Why Reading Aloud to Our Children Will Change Their Lives Forever by Mem Fox

Reading Picture Books with Children: How to Shake Up Storytime and Get Kids Talking About What They See by Megan Dowd Lambert

Redwall series by Brian Jacques

Rocket Says Look Up! by Nathan Bryon, illustrated by Dapo Adeola

Santa Claus: The World's Number One Toy Expert by Marla Frazee

Search for Delicious, The by Natalie Babbitt

Seven Silly Eaters, The by Mary Ann Hoberman, illustrated by Marla Frazee

Sick Day for Amos McGee, A by Philip C. Stead, illustrated by Erin E. Stead

Snowy Day, The by Ezra Jack Keats

Some Babies by Amy Schwartz

Sometimes People March by Tessa Allen

Speaking Our Truth: A Journey of Reconciliation by Monique Gray Smith (Cree, Lakota)

Sylvester and the Magic Pebble by William Steig

The Hate U Give by Angie Thomas

There's Going to Be a Baby by John Burningham, illustrated by Helen Oxenbury

Three Little Pigs, The by Barry Moser

COMBINED MARCH FOR OUR LIVES & WE STAND TOGETHER BOOK LISTS

(referenced in "Reading *Last Stop on Market Street* and Other Diverse Books *with* Children" on page 92)

A Is for Activist by Innosanto Nagara

Adrian Simcox Does NOT Have a Horse by Marcy Campbell, illustrated by Corinna Luyken

All Are Welcome by Alexandra Penfold, illustrated by Suzanne Kaufman

All the World by Liz Garton Scanlon, illustrated by Marla Frazee

Christmas Menorahs, The: How a Town Fought Hate by Janice Cohn, illustrated by Bill Farnsworth

Come With Me by Holly M. McGhee, illustrated by Pascal Lemaître

Day You Begin, The by Jacqueline Woodson, illustrated by Rafael López

Each Kindness by Jacqueline Woodson, illustrated by E. B. Lewis

Elijah's Angel: A Story for Chanukah and Christmas by Michael J. Rosen, illustrated by Aminah Brenda Lynn Robinson

Emma's Poem: The Voice of the Statue of Liberty by Linda Glaser, illustrated by Claire A. Nivola

Grandfather Gandhi by Arun Gandhi and Bethany Hegedus, illustrated by Evan Turk

I Am Human: A Book of Empathy by Susan Verde, illustrated by Peter H. Reynolds

I Can Help by David Hyde Costello

I Have the Right to Be a Child by Alain Serres, illustrated by Aurélia Fronty

I Walk with Vanessa: A Story About a Simple Act of Kindness by Kerascoët

I'm New Here by Anne Sibley O'Brien

Little Book of Little Activists, The by Penguin Books for Young Readers

Malala: Activist for Girls' Education by Raphaële Frier, illustrated by Aurélia Fronty

Peace Book, The by Todd Parr

Rabbit Listened, The by Cori Doerrfeld

Separate Is Never Equal: Sylvia Mendez & Her Family's Fight for Desegregation by Duncan Tonatiuh

Snow in Jerusalem by Deborah da Costa, illustrated by Cornelius Van Wright and Ying-Hwa Hu

Someone New by Anne Sibley O'Brien

Sweet Smell of Roses, A by Angela Johnson, illustrated by Eric Velasquez

This Day in June by Gayle E. Pitman, illustrated by Kristyna Litten

Three Questions, The: Based on a Story by Leo Tolstoy by Jon J. Muth

Trees of the Dancing Goats, The by Patricia Polacco

We March by Shane W. Evans

Why Am I Me? by Paige Britt, illustrated by Selina Alko and Sean Qualls

Yaffa and Fatima: Shalom, Salaam by Fawzia Gilani-Williams, illustrated by Chiara Fedele

BOOK LIST OF SUGGESTIONS TO REPLACE
TO KILL A MOCKINGBIRD
IN MIDDLE-SCHOOL CURRICULUM

(referenced in "Adrian Simcox Is NOT a Mockingbird
[Or, Empathy for Critical Readers]" on page 77)

Fiction

American Street by Ibi Zoboi

Harbor Me by Jacqueline Woodson

Hearts Unbroken by Cynthia Leitich Smith (Muskogee)

Marrow Thieves, The by Cherie Dimaline (Metis)

Mighty Miss Malone, The by Christopher Paul Curtis

*No Crystal Stair: A Documentary Novel of the Life and Work of Lewis
Michaux, Harlem Bookseller* by Vaunda Micheaux Nelson,
illustrated by R. Gregory Christie

Parker Inheritance, The by Varian Johnson

Piecing Me Together by Renée Watson

Poet X, The by Elizabeth Acevedo

White Rose by Kip Wilson

Nonfiction

*Boys Who Challenged Hitler, The: Knud Pedersen and the Churchill
Club* by Phillip Hoose

*Never Caught, the Story of Ona Judge: George and Martha
Washington's Courageous Slave Who Dared to Run Away*
(Young Readers Edition) by Eric Armstrong Dunbar and
Kathleen Van Cleve

Port Chicago 50, The: Disaster, Mutiny, and the Fight for Civil Rights
by Steve Sheinkin

ACKNOWLEDGMENTS

This book would not be without my children. To Rory, Natayja, Emilia, Stevie, Caroline, Jesse, and Zachary: my dearest wish is for you to be happy and us to be close. I'm grateful for all we've shared, including reading memories, and I hope this book serves as a tangible expression of my gratitude and unconditional love. Rory: extra-special thanks for your afterword in your singular voice.

Many others helped bring this book into being, including the writers and illustrators whose books serve as a crucial bonding site for my family. In *this* book, artist Mia Saine's illustrations thrill me with their inviting, empowering, loving interpretations of my words. Thank you from the bottom of my heart. Thanks also to attorney Debbie Orenstein who helped with contract negotiations and is always just plain nice to talk to.

Yolanda Scott and Roger Sutton were two early champions of my writing at Charlesbridge and the *Horn Book*, respectively. Thank you for believing I had something special to say about family reading. Roger: thanks for articulating that belief so well in your foreword. Special thanks to friend and editor Karen Boss, whose ruthless yet sensitive editing cut longer pieces while preserving my voice, and to stellar designer Kristen Nobles.

Melissa Giraud and Andrew Grant-Thomas: EmbraceRace's work fills me with hope. Thank you for your friendship, for inviting me to write, and for permission to share pieces here. Added thanks to the Reading While White team for sharing my writing, too.

I also owe thanks to Eric Carle Museum of Picture Book Art and Simmons University colleagues for supporting my work, chief among them Cathie Mercier and the late Susan Bloom, who were my professors when *I* was a Simmons grad student. I thank all my teachers and librarians for helping me become the reader, writer, and thinker I am. My Simmons students and storytime attendees at the Carle likewise deserve appreciation for showing me books in new ways. I'll add thanks to my children's teachers and librarians, as well as gratitude to Dana Mergendahl and Ramsey Kurdi for coparenting excellence.

Many friends and colleagues provided encouragement, critiques, and support, especially Anna Markus, Breanna McDaniel, Cheryl Bardoe, Lisa Papademetriou, Molly Burnham, and Vicky Smith. My staff at Modern Memoirs, Inc.—Ali de Groot, Nicole Miller, Liz Sonnenberg, and Julie Shively—makes me grateful for our good work and the space it affords me to continue following my path in children's literature.

To my Lambert, Dowd, and St. Marie families, you've shaped me in more ways than I can say. Special thanks for cheering me on: cousin-friends Kevin Lambert and Theresa Schwegel; godparents Hank and Molly Lambert; my kindergarten-teaching aunt, Susan Ellingwood; siblings Sean and Keita Lambert and their families; and parents Ray and Linda Lambert.

And to my husband, Sean St. Marie: amid life's ups and downs, you are my happily ever after. Thank you for your love and unwavering support and for making me believe that "the best is yet to be."